A ~~risk~~ management book (un)like all the others

Clive Martin

First published 2020

By Clive Martin Consulting Limited
12 John Prince's Street
London
W1G 0JR
www.clivemartinconsulting.com
info@clivemartinconsulting.com

Original cover artwork: "Coronavirus – holiday cancelled"
Clive Martin

'The pages race past like the many enjoyable conversations I've had with Clive throughout my career as a colleague, client and friend. The entertaining anecdotes and practical advice he shares in this risk management mystery tour will be insightful for risk professionals and anyone making decisions in business! As he wisely says, risk management needs to change when everything else is changing in the world around us and it's people like Clive who are pushing us in the right direction.'

Colin Gray, Senior Vice President, Risk and Assurance, InterContinental Hotels Group

'Clive's book has a unique, personal style which makes risk management accessible to all through an engaging set of fun life stories, tips and checklists. It 'bridges' non-risk management specialists into the practicalities of 'what to do' and 'how to go about things', which should improve confidence in dealing with risk and assurance.'

Bryan Foss, Independent Director, Visiting Professor Bristol Business School and Co-Founder www.riskcoalition.org.uk

'If you only read one entertaining and possibly even true account of a risk management professional's eventful journey through the risks and opportunities of life and business, make it this one! Adds a splash of memorable colour to an important subject.'

Iain Wright, Chairman, Institute of Risk Management

To Lara, Annabel, Olivia...
...and risk management progress fans, everywhere

PREFACE

I want to help the world be better at taking risks. This book is intended to contribute by reaching out to those who can make a difference but, for whatever reason, have not yet been seduced by more conventional approaches to risk management writing which, when you think about it, is nearly everyone.

I can't help wanting to do this. It's deeply entrenched in me.

Although it was over 30 years prior to the devastating impact of COVID-19, I still remember the first person I ever heard speaking about risk management. There was I - still at school with all the academic motivation of a wet toilet roll - and there was he, the now legendary Professor Gordon Dickson poised at the front of an auditorium full of middle-achieving (at that time... many have gone on to be very successful) school kids.

To look at, Professor Dickson gave off little energy... his large droopy eyes suggesting that the effects of his morning coffee had worn off more than a couple of hours ago.

I must have gone to the open day for the B.A. Risk Management course at what is now Glasgow Caledonian University because when I flicked through the printed prospectus it sounded quite interesting and for some reason it stayed on my ever-decreasing shortlist.

I had a passing affinity with fruit machines (gaming machines) at that time and maybe it was the thought of understanding more about how the odds worked which drew me to it. It might have been that although maybe it was the news coverage I had witnessed recently about the Piper Alpha disaster. Maybe it was coming home from a birthday party only to see the tragic news coverage of The Herald of Free Enterprise capsize. Maybe it was fluctuating fortunes of coal mines, steelworks and certain football clubs at that time. About a decade even earlier, every Scot had learned a risk management lesson from the national football team's Argentinian "misadventure" under Ally MacLeod so maybe it was from those distant days of footballing dreams.

The truth is, I don't really know what it was that eventually brought me to that place but I do know one thing for sure - when Professor Dickson opened his mouth and slow-dripped his dulcet tones on the subject of risk management it changed the direction of my life. Within this seemingly quiet and unassuming man lurked a risk management visionary and genius and those sorts of people can be pretty compelling, can't they?

The things he said and the way he delivered his points to his audience convinced me that I wanted to do this degree course and no other. He sparked my interest with his entertaining stories and analogies and then grounded it all with the prospect of recruiters coming to the degree course to seek graduates.

'Learn how to be a better risk taker and then get hired without too much effort'.

Bingo!

I didn't just submit my application. Oh no... that would not have been trying hard enough. Instead, I took the opportunity to go and see the course organizer and admissions leader to tell him how much I wanted to do this particular degree course above all others and how the subject matter fascinated me.

Looking back on my college days, I maybe came across as a bit too keen to the university staff and my fellow students (because I was always volunteering in the lectures and giving everything I had to the course) but that was just a symptom of me being off on an all-engrossing risk management trajectory which brought out the best in me academically and set me on a course for, even if I do say so myself, making a bit of a splash in some parts of the risk management world.

Of course, one of the problems of listening to someone as eloquent, insightful and logically creative as Professor Dickson is that you don't half miss them when they are no longer there or, more accurately, you yourself have moved on which was the case after graduation a few years later.

When I qualified in risk management which (at least in a structured sense) was actually quite a new concept at the time, I knew my knowledge might be ahead of common practice in many situations but it was still a shock to find out that things we had learned in the first week at college, were being presented as leading-edge thinking in the corporate market four years later. I had plenty to learn about business though so often had to juggle between being an ambitious and capable trainee who knew very little of the real world with being someone who actually knew more than most about how risk and uncertainty could be managed in more effective and efficient ways across organisations. I was a bright, ambitious and capable trainee at Willis, a global blue-chip firm, and I was probably also a bit of a pain in the proverbial to the good people who worked there.

Now, over 30 years on, it still amazes me how little the management of risk has moved on in some places. That's not to say it hasn't changed because the world around us all has changed, big time, since Kylie Minogue (there is more of her in the book) was first in the charts and so of course the management of risk has changed too.

It's just that I can't help feeling that risk management's true potential could be unleashed if today, we had more of the creativity Professor Dickson and his wonderful colleagues showed in the late 80s.

Even during my long stint at EY including nine years as a Partner, I could see that the opportunity for risk management improvement was everywhere in the marketplace but not always particularly obvious to those who had the power, opportunity and motivation to make the change.

Today, around the world, the Covid-19 pandemic has highlighted many continuing 'shortcomings' (we will argue about that later in the book) in peoples' understanding of risk and how it can be managed in a better way. You don't need to look very hard to find some fairly lumpy risk management practice. In fact, you can get a rough idea of things from simply sitting on your sofa and watching TV or reading the news.

It was with all that in mind that I decided to write this book. It's all very well to feel good about articles posted on LinkedIn which get some positive feedback from an echo chamber of like-minded people but that won't make the sort of difference to risk management practice that someone like me has always pushed for. I've pushed for risk management improvement in whatever nature of job role I actually had at different times because it was relevant to them all (client account leader, practice/business leader, program leader, consultant, auditor etc).

'You should write a book about risk management', people kept telling me but for many years I didn't fancy it.

Firstly, I didn't think risk management textbooks sold that many copies so I wasn't sure it would be worth my while financially and secondly, there were already many risk management textbooks in existence ranging from overarching 'Introduction to...' type specimens to very detailed 'deep dives' into specialist areas. I didn't want to write just another textbook on risk management only for it to decay unread on the shelves of professional body libraries and in "rusty" digital folders of electronic readers. Instead, I just focused on trying to make interesting content for LinkedIn by combining lateral thinking and fresh ideas to produce posts and articles - hoping that the mysterious LinkedIn algorithm would spot my talent and push the content out to at least all of my contacts (which of course it very rarely did).

Coincidentally, around the same time that I began to think more seriously about my writing, I compiled a list of celebrities I'd had some sort of personal real-life encounter with during my life. It was for a birthday party quiz and creating the list made me realise just how long it was (there were about 40 or so well-known names on the list). People quite enjoyed hearing the stories about the encounters too. Some of the stories sparked thoughts in me of how to bridge some of the celebrity stories with my thoughts on risk management. Once a bridger, always a bridger.

Then it struck me... although it initially sounded like a terrible idea, I could write a risk management textbook like no other. It would partly be like no other because of the original thoughts and ideas I'd be relaying in it but also because of the celebrity linkages which I hoped would be entertaining and after all, it seemed to me that we have all had (and will continue to have) such misery from Covid-19 that something useful AND fun might be a welcome outlet.

Also, I thought it could provide an opportunity to share some of what was going on in my head at the time I wrote the LinkedIn content. Why had I written these articles and posts? What was it that made me shape them in the way I did and how could all this help take the messages to a new audience... not so much the well-read risk management specialists in our midst but other people who perhaps know a little about formalised risk management but whose experience of it to date had left them a little flat. What if I could ignite something in them in the same way as Professor Gordon Dickson did for me all those years go?

The more I thought about it, the more the 'terrible idea' began to take shape in my head and then one day during the Coronavirus lockdown I decided to start "getting it down on paper" (which is an old-fashioned term for typing it into an iPad Pro which of course was what I actually did). The more I typed and created, the more I realised that a "Risk Management" book for non-specialist risk management folks could simply be described as a "Management book" because it's the business managers that manage risks (well or otherwise) so anything meaningful to do with risk management could/should be of interest to them. By "them", I mean "you".

A few months and some heavy edits later, it finally looked like I might just have something which could appeal to some people as a nice bit of holiday/weekend/commuting reading.

Whether you agree or disagree with the points made in the reference articles or in the tips I've extracted from the celebrity experiences and some personal stories (which are all true), I hope you find the content interesting and that you enjoy reading your new book.

Most of all, I hope you have some fun because life is short, isn't it?

Table of Contents

INTRODUCTION

Hi everybody!

Let's all take risks. Let's make them good ones.

I took a risk writing this book. I like to think of it as smart risk taking. Good for me. Hurrah!

I say I took a risk because this book differs considerably from more established formats for risk management books and, as Burt Bacharach (musical genius) will tell you, it can initially be quite difficult to get other people to accept something which is different to more well-established and familiar patterns... no matter how natural it feels to you.

Most people, when they look it up, are staggered at just how many hits the musical maestro has written - usually for other people to shine by singing them. After becoming a fan of his in the 2010s (a very long time after his songs first became famous) I read his biography and then saw him live in concert in London in 2019. When he played my favourite song of his towards the end of the concert, it was such an amazing moment in time... goosebumps and hairs standing up on the back of my neck, of course. Just awesome.

The thing is, part of his genius was and still is to take songs where you don't think they are going to go next either in pitch or rhythm and that's not a million miles away from what I've attempted to do in this book about risk management.

There, dear reader, the comparison with Burt Bacharach must end because his song-writing success in his 90+ years to date is far in excess of anything you and I can achieve together on risk management by going through this book!

Now with that little diversion, I might have lost some hardcore risk management readers, already but I still have you, my friend and we can make our own music together through this little album of risk management melodies.

Alright, maybe nobody has shut the book yet because even lovers of more traditional risk management textbooks will probably be keen to see how a risk book unlike all the others actually reads. It's not that other risk management textbooks are anything less than good but it is rare for a textbook about risk management to be, how can I say it, *entertaining* in more than just the academic sense and, for some, that might take a bit of getting used to.

Let me put it this way - if you don't like the sound of what you've just read then there is still time to put the book down and slowly walk away. Count to ten as you go and breathe deeply... do not lash out. We don't need to talk of this ever again.

To *all* those who remain, regardless of background diversity factors including risk management orientation, I say 'hello good people, friends and respected colleagues - come in'!

Welcome to a ~~risk~~ management textbook (un)like all the others.

Yep, I've deliberately put a strikethrough on the word risk because I like to think that this is really a management book about risk... which will hopefully tickle the fancy of an even more inclusive group of good people who are interested in how humans grapple with uncertainty.

Those who already know me, professionally, will tell you that I'm not averse to some creativity when it comes to delivering content and I think you will find more of it than you might expect for a book about ~~risk~~ management.

That's because I'm trying to appeal to those who are not already steeped in risk management and at the same time offer something of interest to those who are. I'm trying to improve the management of risk by everyone – even if it is via one anecdote at a time!

You can read the chapters of this book in any order you wish as although there are some unavoidable linkages due to the subject matter, the main points in each are essentially standalone so the flexibility is for you to use as you see fit. I did consider grouping the chapters into more conventional risk management headings but not only was this a bit tricky (because real life risk management lessons tend not to sit neatly in single silos), it would also make it look a bit more like all other risk management books which, dear reader, you will have gathered by now was something I set out to actively avoid.

If you are totally new to risk management in a formal sense then you might like to temporarily skip to the Formula One articles first (after Kylie Minogue because everyone will read that one first, I'm sure) but if you already have some reasonable understanding of risk management then the order presented might work fine for you. It's your call though and I'm assured that even some of the A-list celebrities in chapter headings and/or making cameo I appearances in other chapter anecdotes are not too bothered if you read them first or last... so you don't have to worry about that!

There are no true guarantees in this world (even taxes, if you look closely enough) but if you offer up some of your precious time (in a series of moments and places which suits you) to browsing these pages of what must surely be 'indisputable' wisdom then I promise you I will either give something interesting or entertaining in return.

And if you think there might be some ambiguity in that last paragraph then you'd be right. Also, if you are worried about the last sentence starting with "And" then this book might not be for you either.

Right, buckle up, Amigos... and let's get ready for a gallop through some saucy (in the North American meaning of the word) risk management lessons from my years in the game.

Let's go!

1

KYLIE MINOGUE – I should be so lucky

So, there she was all alone... her face two feet away from mine, looking into my eyes wondering who was going to make the first move.

Before I go any further, I should probably put some context around this.

I always knew I'd meet Kylie Minogue... ever since she switched from primetime television actress to pop star (and subsequently "The Queen of Pop") in the later 80s, I knew I'd meet her at some point. Maybe it was that my frame of reference for big city night life was Glasgow and I had no real understanding of how huge London was, so I thought I'd just see her in a nightclub or something.

Anyway, I was moving to London and assumed I'd see her at some stage.

I should just add (in case anyone gets the wrong idea) that I didn't come to London in search of Kylie Minogue! I came to London to pursue my career in risk management and, in retrospect, to meet my wonderful wife.

Anyway, quite a chunk of time later, I was coming back from a daytrip to Paris (as you do). The purpose of my visit was to introduce myself to a possible new client and the meeting had gone really well from my perspective.

On the return Eurostar journey I was very busy typing up notes and working out what to do next in terms of building the relationship with the potential client.

There had actually been a bit of a mix up with the tickets that day with the result that I had ended up in a carriage which was neither economy class nor business class.

Oh no, none of that rubbish thank you very much. I was living the big time now (even if it was by accident) so found myself in the opulent luxury of some sort of premier class (which I'd never even heard of on the Eurostar before).

However it had come about, I was glad of the elbow space as I typed away like a frenzied pianist being given the hurry-up by a sweaty conductor.

Although engrossed in my work, I was aware of a large gentleman doing something similar further down the carriage and occasionally the only other occupant of the carriage wafted past me down the aisle. Purely due to the passing proximity to my downward gaze, I had clocked the fact that she was wearing blue denims and a gingham shirt but that was the only thing I had noted because I was, after all, coming back to the London office with a success story and wanted to think about how best to leverage the meeting I'd just had.

The journey passed by really quickly. In reality it took about three hours I think but it went in a flash from my perspective and as the train rolled its way into Waterloo station (as it did in those days), I packed everything away and stood up to walk down the aisle towards the front of the train.

As I did so, the big guy in front did the same but hadn't finished packing his briefcase so proceeded to block the aisle meaning I couldn't move forward. Neither could the lady on the opposite side of the aisle as her exit was now blocked too.

She was kneeling on the seat by the aisle and I was standing two feet away. For one very brief moment, she looked at me straight in the eyes and I did the same with her... wondering who was going to make the first move - to get further down the aisle, that is. Well what did you think I meant?

I remember thinking at the time that she was quite attractive and that she looked a little bit like Kylie Minogue but as I said, she had jeans on instead of hotpants so I didn't make the full connection.

The large gentleman moved down the aisle and I was now free to follow him, which I did.

It was only when I got off the train and was going underneath the platform towards customs that I realized that it might actually have been Kylie Minogue after all but she was nowhere to be seen.

Then, as I approached the gates, she suddenly appeared before me, slipped through the gates (I can't remember if she did a spin or not) and was immediately swept up by a burly gentleman dressed all in black and wearing some form of earpiece. I was then aware of the station security staff all pointing at her and nodding to each other.

Yep, I had basically spent three hours in an empty train carriage with Kylie Minogue and not realized it was her!

People subsequently told me that she was seeing a French boyfriend at the time and had a sponsorship deal with Eurostar which possibly explained things.

What are my risk management tips from this long-anticipated and almost totally missed encounter?

Remember you don't know what is going on in peoples' personal lives.

It turns out, she had cancer. Although the news hadn't broken at the time, I think she was probably aware of it and I wonder what was going through her head during that journey and how it must have affected her.

Looking back, it was quite an interesting exercise to consider what I might have said to her if I had realized it was indeed Kylie Minogue when I was essentially alone with her. When I told the tale to friends, they came up with quite an imaginative set of chat up lines, I can assure you!

If you strip away the novelty of celebrity status though and consider that she was a real person who had probably only recently received some very upsetting news (which was not the first upsetting news she had received in her life), the range of one-liner introductions takes on a whole new shape - one which is far more sensitive to the feelings of the other fellow human being and one which, in retrospective, would have been far more likely to produce a positive outcome.

We all know, but sometimes forget, that people are humans too and everyone's got "issues" in their personal lives.

We know this about people we are closest to at work because of the impromptu discussions we have with them and sometimes the formal structures of managerial or counselling relationships bring these issues to light. What we sometimes forget is that everybody else has them too - the people we are not that close to.

Those interested in good risk taking will know that influencing other people is usually an important component of being successful. Whether you are helping someone take the right risks, stopping them taking the wrong ones, or taking those risks yourself, the outcomes are often influenced directly or indirectly by other people who have things going on outside of their work persona and which, directly or indirectly, consciously or sub-consciously affects how they operate.

One of the things about dealing with risk is that conversations and discussions about it can take place at a time of heightened emotion. Whether you are trying to challenge someone on a certain aspect of risk or trying to "bat off" somebody who has challenged you, these interactions can generate quite a bit of emotion as either side can feel that their competence is being questioned and the stakes can be quite high.

Of course, there is often no way of knowing for sure what issues the other person is going through in their personal lives - unless you are psychic, or the other person happens to be one of those who post everything about themselves on social media.

I'm not suggesting that you should try and understand the detail of what's going on in the other person's personal life (for one thing, you'd quite possibly end up taking on half their emotional strain yourself and that's not something to make a habit of doing if you want to stay standing).

What I am suggesting though is that in the big moments of challenge/ defence (which should be a key feature of healthy risk management in an organization) it's worth remembering that the human being you are dealing with is not a robot - even if they sometimes give the impression that they are, which some do. It's not always about cold logic when feelings and emotional context are in the driving seat.

Adopting a more human and humane approach to dealing with risk issues might just lead to a better result (which could be better risk taking) because the challenge would be better made and better received.

How you do that - how you calibrate behaviour, language and degrees of challenge/ defence - is another subject but keeping in mind that the other person is a real person and whatever their work/ public persona might be dealing with moments of significant stress or trauma, is a good first step in the right direction.

9

Sometimes, it is possible to get so engrossed in a recent success that you fail to notice the opportunity which is in front of you.

The really big picture is that I possibly didn't miss any sort of "opportunity" from my encounter with Ms Minogue. Sure, at a micro level, I missed an opportunity to say at least something to her and hear her say something to me. At best, this might have resulted in some sort of awkward chat.

Nevertheless, the point about being so happy with a recent success that you miss something new has lots of applications in risk management, the potential ramifications of which can sometimes extend far beyond the most likely parameters of my encounter with one of pop music's biggest international superstars.

You might have taken a big risk in your organization which has paid off - you won that tender, the public love your new product, your aggressive takeover bid has been reluctantly accepted, or your post-merger integration has produced the promised benefits (well it does happen sometimes you know!). Whatever your success was, you can certainly enjoy it but don't take your eye off the ball because you might just miss an opportunity to take an even bigger risk which has just come along offering a bucket load of opportunity.

Of course, it's not all about the positive. You can be so busy celebrating or acting on a recent success that you miss the emergence of a big wave of riskiness. Complacency is probably not the right word to use here because that would imply some form of invincibility syndrome and although that is something important to watch for, it's not what I'm focusing on here.

Rather than complacency, it's probably more 'distraction'. In this case, you're not being distracted by a bad thing... you are being distracted by a good thing which causes you not to give as much attention as you would otherwise have given to the chance to deal with a different good thing or bad thing.

In other words, it's important stay alert to the speculative and pure risks that arise in pursuit of opportunity, including right after you've just had a cracking success.

Football pundits used to joke that the Scotland football team 'had the worst possible start to the game... they went 1-0 up!' implying that the period immediately after taking the lead could be the most dangerous in terms of inward threat. It's that sort of thing I'm trying to address with this tip.

Staying alert to uncertainty is sometimes easier to do following an event with a bad outcome than it can be when everything has just gone 'hunky dory' so the tip is to stay focused in all situations which is king of obvious now I've said it... but if only someone had reminded me of it in the heat of the moment on that train!

Occasionally, the "aisle blocker" might actually be doing you a favour because it gives you the opportunity to look around.

Is that a metaphor for people that slow you down? Yes, it is.

Okay, to be fair, most people that block the aisles on trains are really a pain. It's even worse on airplanes... especially those full of hand luggage only customers at airports where the taxi service is limited. I can recall several occasions where what would have otherwise been a 30 mins taxi queue saving dash down the aisle was scuppered by someone rolling out of their seat in front of me and slowly fumbling to find some of their missing hand luggage at the back of the overhead lockers.

In a work sense, our progress can be hampered in many other ways. Whether it is the red tape of bureaucracy, the unexpected challenge of our numbers or assumptions, or the inability of clients to secure the final stage of budgetary approval, things can get in our way and slow us down.

Maybe you are the one blocking the aisle for now because you feel the protagonists of change have missed something or not yet given enough consideration to an aspect of risk.

It can feel very frustrating for progress to be blocked when we just want to get on with it.

There will be times when the blocking is simply a nonsense - adding no value and providing no opportunity for anything useful. That could be bad risk management or bad management more broadly.

However, there will also be occasions when the temporary blocking provides an opportunity to have a bit of a look around.

Looking around might do nothing other than increase our confidence that we were right all along and that of course can be valuable in itself, can't it? You know, double-checking, consideration of further evidence, checking out alternative opportunities which confirm your original intention was the best plan.

Looking around can also result in a change of direction though, even if it is only a beneficial detour to the same ultimate destination. Maybe you will see something from a different perspective, gain greater recognition of the true confidence levels you should have in your original plan, or just think a bit more about the effort which is going to be needed for ultimate success.

So, the next time this happens to you, by all means allow yourself to feel some of the frustration caused by the blocker but, if you can, also just take those moments, days, weeks, months to look around as you never know what you might see when you do. It probably won't be Kylie Minogue but you never know!

2

BINARY STATEMENTS LEAD TO MIXED MESSAGES

LinkedIn article:

This seemingly paradoxical hypothesis is getting plenty of trial time at the moment: "When will the tests be ready?"; "How many people will contract the virus?"; "Do you accept that you did the wrong thing in using those tactics?"; "When will this all be over?"; are examples of the type of closed questions which prompt binary answers.

The push for binary answers encourages similarly binary responses; "It will be X", "There will be X ready by YY/YY/YY".

Seldom, do you witness questions or responses which deal with probabilities. "Well, we believe there is a 60% chance that X tests will be ready by YY/YY/YY, and 90% chance that they will be ready by ZZ/ZZ/ZZ".

Why is that?

I wonder why we are starved of such enlightening enhancements to the communications streams we witness and sometimes participate in.

Some people will say it's because "Joe Public doesn't understand probabilities". This is of course a sweeping generalization. Plenty of the population understand betting odds which look similar to me.

There is arguably an educational deficit when it comes to risk and associated probabilities. It seems there is an inability in the media and in many other types of organizations to deal with uncertainty and probabilities... it's only whether you would class this as an "educational deficit" or not which seems to be in question.

Some blinkered quants will say the lack of richness in the discussions about risk is down to lack of data. "How can you say something is X% probable if you have no data to prove it?" they will state. Such a purist approach is understandable but not particularly useful if you are on the front line because it encourages you to then make binary statements (which will often be no more reliable due to lack of data).

How come we can make binary assertions without data but nothing on probabilities of less that 100%?

Is it all that bad to make estimates without data? I don't mean reckless estimates which ignore data. I mean in situations where reliable data is unavailable but you still need to make decisions. Using intuition and guestimates might actually be helpful if one is communicative about the logic. "Well, the reason I'm doing this is on the presumption that there is a 50% chance it will be no more than X and 90% chance it will be no more than Y" could be a simple example of a statement which is more sensible than binary assertions such as "We are doing this because we are right" (which is essentially the approach being taken by some at the moment). If people can understand the basis on which you are operating and you make it clear that you might change direction (if better data actually comes to light or you just change your mind) then they should be more understanding of changes in direction.

Maybe it is the legal specialists who are advising that any suggestion that things are other than binary is less risky than accepting that there is uncertainty and that the real world plays out through statistical distributions that humans don't yet have a complete handle on. If that was true, it would be an interesting situation for us all to be in – maybe we'd all end up making binary statements all the time and imagine what kind of a world that would be.

So binary statements are made here, there and everywhere and the result is mixed messages because a statement about X being ready by Y is different to statement that Z will probably be available by Y and nobody is asking or answering questions in public which deal with probabilities and statistical distributions.

Come on, we can do this!

Come on, we can have mature conversations about risk – surely. Although I have no statistically significant data sets to work with, I've written this article because currently I feel approximately 99% confident that we could have, but only about 10% confident that we will have albeit about 40% confident that we will make some small steps forward.

There... you understand the relationship between these last three "guestimates? and you at least can work out from them why I've written this article. Maybe you could cope with some less binary and more probability-based messages from government and others after all? Of course, you could. I hope we get it.

The clue to my rationale for writing this article is of course contained in the penultimate paragraph where I lay out some probabilities for progress in the maturity of dialogue about risk. You can see that I am very confident in the opportunity for progress (although those of you who really get it will already have spotted that I put it at 99% rather than total certain at 100%).

The pessimism in the other two numbers is plain to see, isn't it? Put another way, without numbers, at the time I wrote this article I thought it very unlikely that we would see significant progress and more likely than not we won't see small steps forward either... at least in the short term.

Blimey, that's quite a bleak outlook on this subject isn't it? Where did that come from?

Well, it probably came from watching too much television news coverage during the lockdown. Lots of things can come from that, including an increased waistline, but I won't go into those other things right now. The thing I want to focus on is the immaturity (and I use that word advisedly) of the discussion.

What I could see, hear and read was dialogue about one of the greatest threats to humankind ever to bless our blue planet. The terror of the infectiousness and deadliness of the virus did not sound good. Questions, dear reader, needed to be asked and in the UK we had our finest politicians and media interviewers all lining up to provide leadership and shed light on this black peril.

Whether shyly or with verbal aggression, interviewers wanted answers to binary questions and whether gingerly or with gusto, politicians gave them the soundbites that everyone needed to be reassured.

Except they didn't.

People didn't get the information they needed to understand the risk and gauge appropriate action accordingly. They did however get sweeping generalisations which were sometimes useful as a guide to action but possibly got in the way of true understanding.

I made the comparison with betting odds in the article because it's a nonsense to say that Joe Public won't understand probabilities (and therefore shouldn't be fed them) and yet they are allowed to place bets which use estimated probabilities as a guide to risk levels. This is particularly true for spread bets on things like total

17

numbers of goals scored or total count of numbers on back of goal scorers' jerseys etc.

Okay, I know not everyone understands betting odds and I will also accept that some (indeed many) don't understand probabilities but why should that stop the information becoming available for those who do understand it and, crucially, for those who could understand it if they had a bit more practice?

Maybe dialogue about probability distributions and the associated curves would have distracted people from understanding the message about 'flattening the curve' which was of course not a probability curve at all.

I sometimes began to wonder what would happen if the different probabilities associated with different degrees of impact were released?   Without questioning the obvious talent of media personnel and politicians, I couldn't help wondering if they, as individuals, would have the knowledge to be able to deal with them.

To be clear, this wasn't a new line of thinking for me which was only brought on by the Coronavirus. I like listening to "In our time" on the BBC and truly admire Melvyn Bragg's ability to navigate such a wide range of intellectually fascinating subjects.   I will admit the panellists lose me from time to time and I either hit rewind on my iPhone or just accept that it's something I'm not going to grasp (this time around).   On topics which deal with complex probabilities though, I'm not always convinced that Melvyn understands it (I apologise unreservedly Mr Bragg if you always do).   He doesn't have to fully understand it though in order to chair the discussion in the same way Chairs of Boards of Directors don't always need to understand everything to do their job (although they do need to understand everything well enough).

Anyway, I digress... my point is that I've often observed situations where the dialogue around risk levels could be more mature (ie probabilistic etc) but instead gets stuck in usual ways of operating meaning that confident assertions that things will/ won't be done by a certain date, rule the roost.

It's the same on many major change projects. If you've ever been closely involved in a major change project you'll recognize program updates proudly asserting that everything is "on track" (which is usually green).

'Oh yes... nothing to see here, Batman, everything is fine and on schedule. We have a list of risks somewhere in the deck but they are all being managed [by which they probably mean controlled] so nothing to worry about. Now let's move on to the next agenda item which is the team's compensation and bonus arrangements'.

How simplistic is that? It's sad to say that on-track usually means 'everything that was supposed to have been done by now has been completed' which is of course a million miles away from saying we are on track for on-time and on-budget completion, isn't it?

It's the way things are often done though, and we know that our old nemesis, corporate history (the way we've always done it in the past) can seriously get in the way of advancement in program management.

Some organisations have thankfully wised up to this, asking programs to provide forward-looking probabilistic estimates of the chances of on-time success of workstreams and the program overall. In those situations, anyone proudly proclaiming 100% guarantee of on-time success, is suspected as trying to hide something. For those organisations, it doesn't always matter if the probabilities cannot be calculated with much accuracy - what's more important is the acceptance of uncertainty and the maturity to be able to have a dialogue about the risk levels, appetite for them, and any consequent action to take less or more of it.

Of course, to have a mature conversation, mature input is needed from more than one party. Imagine what would happen if a politician tried to explain probabilities in a more sophisticated way but the media couldn't or wouldn't cope with it and instead demanded binary answers to its binary questions. It would probably end badly for the politician and that would be a pity because, say what you like about politicians, it would be an ironic shame if in the desire to shed more light on the actual truth they were prevented from doing so by the media.

In other words, you can't be unilateral in the drive to be more insightful on risk levels... you need others to be willing and able to work with you.

Although I did well in statistical analysis at university (I'm pretty sure I got 100% in my second year exam on it) and have maintained good understanding of statistical analysis ever since proudly working for many years with a large number of actuaries (which is not easy for anyone except other actuaries), I know there is more I could learn. Basic Bayesian can only get you so far (although in the land of the blind, that can seem to be quite a long way down the road).

Maybe we all need to gear up on this? Maybe we could all do a little bit better?

The thing is, we need to start somewhere else we are stuck in the endless cycle of doing what we've always done and wondering why it's not leading to more mature conversations about risk.

Where do we get our education from on this, though? After all, not everyone wants to go and study a degree in risk management. Should we start with the young and build more of it into compulsory education so that our citizens of tomorrow (and today) are better equipped to understand uncertainty in the world?

I don't think I know the answer but the blended learning opportunities that exist today ranging from classroom study through instructional YouTube videos to sophisticated online learning mechanisms give us plenty of options.

Will we want to do it, though? Hmm. That could be a tricky one to answer for some but if Coronavirus highlighted the deficit in our dialogue on such a massive scale then maybe future challenges of an even bigger scale (eg global warming) might just make it worth everyone's while.

To summarise the risk management lessons from this article, I'd say the main ones are:
- Binary statements on risk can lead to mixed messages.
- Probability based methods are more insightful and increasingly used by the general public (betting odds)
- The way we've always done it can seriously get in the way of risk management progress
- Mature conversations about risk cannot be had unilaterally
- The virus has reminded us that there are some very big risks to humanity out there which would benefit from improved management through better risk management education

3

DIGITAL ISN'T ALWAYS BINARY AND OTHER MATURE CONVERSATIONS ABOUT RISK

LinkedIn article:

Immature conversations about risk are prevalent in today's society. Whether it be in politics or in business, it feels like we are immature when it comes to discussing uncertainty.

It doesn't have to be that way.

The drive for binary-type "it is or it isn't", "yes or no" responses to questions about uncertainty comes at a cost – typically resulting in a lack of understanding about the true nature of the uncertainty and the opportunity it presents. Why do we do that when we should all know that risks tend to be best characterised by distributions rather than sweeping descriptors of a binary nature?

I can see it in political interviews. I witness it in Board meetings (and sub-committee meetings). I encounter it Steering Group meetings for major programmes. Corporate transaction activity is not averse to it either. Annual Reports & Accounts are sometimes manifestations of the problem too. The opportunity for progress seems to be everywhere.

If we could have more mature conversations about risk it might:

1. Help us (business people, politicians, everyone) take better steps now to deal with global warming, ageing populations and gambling addictions

2. Help us be more confident in the likely success of business, political strategies and major programs and smarter in our approach to agility
3. Help us avoid making guarantees and promises that might not be kept, thus improving trust and true confidence

Can you imagine being able to place greater trust in management information because it was more transparent on risks and smarter on how risks and issues were escalated and priorities set in response?

Can you imagine being able to have faith that statements about risk levels would be met with mature and proportionate responses from investors, regulators, employee groups and other stakeholders?

The good news is, we can move in that direction but if it is such a good thing to pursue then what would actually bring about improvement i.e. more mature dialogue?

We can't just wave a magic wand and expect dialogue to mature overnight after being the way it has been for so long. Also, a unilateral approach would be crazy for any individual person or company. All stakeholders (or at least enough of them) need to be reliable when it comes to having a mature conversation about the true nature of risks and uncertainties.

I suppose that's one of the things that make it difficult.

Education seems important. I don't just mean improving the quality of education in schools and universities about the nature of uncertainty and how it affects so many things, bringing opportunity to exploit and risks to be managed. I think we all need more education on risk and especially how to deal with risks which relate to our changing world like, for example, the non-binary nature of the upsides and downsides presented by digital (if you'll pardon the "binary" pun).

Whether it be about truly understanding risk ourselves or influencing/ nudging/ strongly encouraging others to be adopt a more mature approach to dealing with it, the opportunity to make progress through some form of education, backed up with practical experience of how things can be better is clear.

Maybe we will miss the boat. Maybe humans don't have the capacity or desire to have economic dialogue about risk. Maybe it scares us all too much which is why we prefer the "tell me it's certain" approach to politics and business.

Then again, maybe we can do this – one step at a time. Maybe we can take the opportunity to improve discussion about risk by emphasising the stochastic nature of most risks at every opportunity (even if they are difficult to quantify with precision). Maybe sparks of courage and competence will raise the game at the expense of some in the short term but ultimately for the benefit of everyone.

Come on, we can do this.

A few weeks after I wrote this article, I was watching a television interview with the UK Chancellor at the time, Rishi Sunak. Don't worry, dear reader, I'm not going to get political... and I'll keep my thoughts about the Monster Raving Loony party to myself.

The BBC Breakfast interviewer asked a perfectly reasonable question about "what would happen if...." and although I can't remember fully, it was something to do with the possibility that certain lockdown restrictions might not be lifted after all on a certain date. Or maybe it was something about extension of the furlough scheme, or holiday destinations being added to the quarantine list etc.

For the purposes of my point below, it doesn't really matter!

Keep in mind that this was in the middle (I hope at the time of writing) of the coronavirus lockdown at a point where things looked like they were regaining some structure but there was still a lot of uncertainty around.

So, "What would happen if...?" was the question.

The chancellor responded; "I don't think it would be helpful to comment on a hypothetical situation..."

Eh?

I nearly spat out my cornflakes and thought to myself "Let me get this straight, the country is struggling to grapple with the chaos that coronavirus has inflicted and our Chancellor is not prepared or ready to comment on one perfectly feasible scenario?"

Eh? Eh? (that's a double Eh? reader which is phrase I've just invented to be a verbal version of a 'double take' look). Grammar police... save yourself the trouble and just make a donation to charity.

"You really don't think it would be helpful to comment on something which could well happen next week and people could prepare for it now if they knew what you would do if and when it did?"

Sometimes, words just aren't enough to describe the feeling you get when people cop out of addressing risk properly.

I know where that sort of response comes from, of course. I think it is standard political media training to reel out that response when asked a question about what could happen in the future.

"No, no... there can't be any other possible outcomes, the future will be exactly as I've described it and it's not going to help anyone to talk about anything otherwise."

That's the kind of thing they always say and I can see how in some situations it will be useful - especially if the interviewer is adopting an immature, binary approach to his/her questioning. It keeps things much simpler to say something along those lines.

We were in the middle of a crisis though and it might just have helped people to plan if those with power talked about a few quite possible scenarios so that the public, including business leaders, could get ready with their response as the true future emerged. It struck me that to use that phrase given where we were was a classic example of immature risk dialogue at a time when the public want something else.

What if he said, "well if that happens then we would probably do this but there is also the chance that other factors might means that we do something else instead? Overall though, we think there is only about a 20% chance of that scenario actually occurring"?

Could we cope with that? Keep in mind that the American method of presenting a weather forecast with "x% chance of rain" is yet to make it onto UK channels although many people are now getting their pluvious probabilistic fixes from apps now which do contain the feature! Why? It's because people find it useful so come on, let's have a bit more probabilistic action in our current affairs media.

The tips from this article can be summarised as:

- More mature and probabilistic conversations about risk would be helpful in many ways
- We can take the opportunity for better education about risk in our changing world
- All stakeholders need to be reliable when it comes to mature conversations about risk and uncertainty

4

LinkedIn article:

If effective strategy execution is key then who do you have doing the driving and how are they? Oh, and do they drive like Uncle Silo?

The other day, I was driving along a busy road. It was one of those fast three-lane roads which looks like a motorway but isn't. Anyway, the car in front suddenly swerved to the left and then corrected itself. Then it swerved to the right and partially into another lane before correcting itself again.

This pattern continued for two or three iterations and I found it unnerving even by my own experiences. I was once following another driver to find our villa on holiday when he swerved off the road and into a ditch. No, I didn't follow him into the ditch and yes nobody was hurt in the making of this anecdote.

I have some scary reference points but I looked more closely through the back window of his car and the driver was trying to read something on his center console. Every time he looked down to read it, he swerved quite badly. I flashed my lights to get him to stop but he didn't even notice.

What an irresponsible person. We could do without that sort of dangerous, selfish and reckless behavior, couldn't we?

Anyway, enough of the rant. A few days later down by the seaside, I started to think about driving in an organizational context. I don't mean commercial lorries etc – I mean those implementing strategy i.e. driving the business.

"Understand your <u>drivers</u> not just your drivers"

To what extent does good or bad driving matter in that context? We all know that strategic failure is often about poor execution (bad driving) rather than a bad strategy per se so it seems it must be critically important.

While walking along an empty beach in the rain (don't worry I had my raincoat on), I tried to develop the analogy further in my head and tried to think of corporate equivalents to the following:

- Would you care more about bad driving if you own the vehicle (as an example, a corporate equivalent of that might be "does employee ownership influence the quality of strategy execution")?
- Would you care more about bad driving if you were actually in the car with the bad driver (if you have proximity to danger, possibly regulatory, would it make you care more about strategic execution)?
- Would you tolerate bad driving if you were in a less-safe car without so many controls and safety features?
- Would you care more about bad driving if you were on a road that was unpredictable?
- Who says what constitutes bad driving, anyway – what is it?
- Do you know how good a driver you really are?

"...opportunities to improve the strategic aspects of people risk can be clear to everyone who looks ahead."

- Would you do more about stopping bad driving if you knew the driver?
- Would you care more about bad driving if timing (i.e. speed) was critically important for what you were trying to achieve?
- To what extent should you tolerate the mistakes of learner drivers?
- Would you report dangerous drivers if it was easier to do so?
- Would you care more about bad driving if you had no access to insurance?
- Does bad driving matter if you are surrounded by other bad drivers who all expect each other to drive badly?
- Should others care about the extent to which you care about the quality of driving?
- How much ($) would you be prepared to spend to improve your own driving and the driving of others around you?

The list could go on even for this simple analogy. Were you able to think of corporate equivalents to each of the above? It's worth re-reading the list and having a good think about it if you didn't first time around (I'll bet most of you didn't!).

Thinking that peoples' corporate answers to the questions might start with "it all depends…" I threw a pebble into the sea and decided it was too difficult to work through this analogy fully, for a short article.

Clambering back up the beach, other thoughts about corporate driving raced through my mind.

Is it enough to leave the driving to others? If the journey is for your benefit then do you have any sort of responsibility for the driving? How far should business leaders go to oversee and monitor those driving the implementation of strategy for them? How utilitarian should we be? Does the quality of the driving matter as long as the end goal is reached?

Different people in differing situations will probably have differing views on what is the right thing to do in relation to these aspects of strategy execution just as different people will have different views on whether it was sensible to go to the beach in the rain.

"Some of the best books on... strategy mapping are quite quiet on managing risk..."

As I walked over the last crunchy pebbles and onto the soft, silent grass I thought about two actions for addressing the challenge.

1.   Understand your *drivers* not just your drivers

Everyone knows it is important to understand the drivers of your strategy but what about the ***drivers***....i.e. the people doing it? My own view is that it is important to understand your drivers... how are they? They are people and although they might also be working with machines, they are human so it would seem sensible to ensure that aspects associated with being human are properly included in strategy mapping.

Strategy maps will usually address a whole host of different strategic drivers and will typically include something on people. "Recruit best talent" "motivated workforce" "suitably skilled people" are examples of items that might typically be expected. Going beyond that though, effective mapping needs to lay out how these things might be achieved given that people are human and not machines and this aspect is not always as well developed as it could be.

People are risky and they don't always do what you think or want. Their behaviour is best influenced if it can somehow be understood to begin with. Although some might say it is impossible to fully understand and predict behaviour, tools continue to emerge (supported by very big data) which improve the degree to which we can be at least partly confident about doing so. It seems to follow then that strategy mapping should lead to the use of some of those tools and data in a structured way.

2. Give your drivers a reference framework for dealing with uncertainty.

Although the strategic destination (short or long term) is often clear for an organization, there will be uncertainties associated with the journey and the drivers will need a reference framework for dealing with them. Some would say that good corporate driving in a rapidly changing world is less about where you are aiming and more about your ability to deal with the challenges that will pop up along the way. Those challenges might also change your goals and so it is important to remain open and flexible to that wherever possible.

What could such a reference framework for dealing with uncertainty look like? Well, it would certainly contain all the basics associated with effective risk management. The way in which they are shaped and applied will of course vary depending on the nature of the industry and strategic challenge being addressed but as so many industries are impacted by digital shifts and the use of very big data that tools and training specifically developed for managing uncertainties in that field are likely to be in high demand (subject to pricing!).

However, some of the best books on strategy maps and strategy mapping are quite quiet on managing risk and I've often wondered why that is.

It could be our old problematic relative, Uncle Silo. You know, the fact that many corporate disciplines still operate pretty much in isolation of one another when some cross-specialism approaches might produce a better result. Uncle Silo is human as well though so you can't just expect him to behaviour differently because you say so – changing behaviour is usually more complicated than that.

Conclusion

There can be no doubt that significant progress has been made in some industries in terms of risk professionals actively contributing to strategy setting and planning through strategic risk assessments etc but I think it safe to say that, in general, more progress can be made here – especially when it comes to people risk. Analogies (such

> as the car driving/ corporate driving) one above can help people understand why people risk is worthy of more consideration. Good driving is perhaps relative and in the eye of the beholder but opportunities to improve the strategic aspects of people risk can be clear to everyone who looks ahead.

It's interesting how witnessing someone driving badly and, in extreme cases, crashing in front of you trigger thoughts about vulnerability and uncertainty.

Although it's a little underplayed in the article, the holiday anecdote about the driver who said "follow me" and then at high speed lurched into a ditch was pretty frightening... not least because we had kids in the back and of course had to stop by the side of the road to check if the driver was okay. We were certainly in a mild state of shock which is just as well because it got us through the rest of the journey and it was only after the journey had ended that the true gravity of what we had witnessed kicked in. Needless to say, the other driver shuffled away pretty quickly after leading us to our destination, perhaps in fear that we might smell his breath. A benefit of technology and satnavs in particular is that nowadays we don't need drivers who might have come straight from a drinking session showing us the way from airports.

When I got onto writing about drivers of strategy (i.e. the people involved) in strategic execution, I thought about it from their point of view. I've often been one of them too of course so this was actually quite easy to do. I started to think about the strategies that I had created, mapped and implemented for the business/practices I had run and how it felt to be the one primarily responsible for understanding and dealing with the uncertainties associated with them.

Getting beyond the 'what am I?' and 'what am I doing?' line of questioning and into the 'how am I?' space was key and that's what I was getting at in the article... people are human and it could be useful to know how they are if you want to be confident in them delivering in the way you envisaged.

Of course, how I think I am might not be the same as how you think I am or, in the case of the point I made in the article, how other current/possible sources of data think I am.

Some new sources of workplace data sprung up during Covid-19 providing input on how people were physically e.g. temperature sensing scanners etc and these in some instances were linked directly to risk control measures such as security gates etc so that automatic blocking could be instigated in the event that the sensors thought someone might have the virus.

On the mental side of things, lots of new technologies were emerging well before the virus ranging from psychometric type tests to social media scanners and even voice recognition/interpretation technology.

It felt to me that those possibilities could and perhaps should get more attention in strategy documents - especially those relating to mapping and implementation.

Beyond that aspect of people risk, broader risk management improvement could be made by those driving strategy if they were given more of a framework for coping with uncertainty, or so I argued in the article.

I often wondered why so many strategy documents of the past contained so very little in relation to risk and uncertainty before I realized the reasons was that they just hadn't done it that way in the past.

There's the curse of being a good risk management specialist - your visions for a better world nearly always require people to do things in ways other than that which they have been used to for decades.

You know what silos can be like in some organisations... the walls go up and the shutters come down when someone from another division wants to come and play in their back yard. This is often especially true when the visitor "would prefer it if things were done differently around here".

I was quite pleased with the words I found for 'our old problematic relative, Uncle Silo'. I wanted to imply some familiarity (hence the 'Uncle' bit) but also to point out that we really have to deal with the problem of organizational silos if we are to optimize risk management at a strategic level to deal with the big changes happening in our world which don't respect organizational boundaries.

Reference frameworks for dealing with uncertainty (risk) across organizational silos are critical because they provide the language and the platform for those previous silos to, dare I say it, collaborate and agree overall risk management priorities rather than silo by silo priorities.

Being right is the easy bit though and the effort involved in positioning, nudging, and convincing others to work in a different way can be more challenging than you might think for CROs and CEOs.

Remember, very few organizational entities need to operate across all other departments in the way that Risk functions do but since I wrote the article, I've realized that Risk functions and "digital functions' might actually make for a good cross-silo working alliance because digital functions are typically trying to bring about new ways of working across older silos too. They could go hand in hand together pretty nicely but I bet in many cases they don't because neither side have yet realized the opportunity they are missing to lead the way on operating across boundaries together.

So all in all, I think I'd add that last point to the tips in the article such that the three tips from this chapter are:

- How people are deserves some proper attention in strategy mapping and implementation
- The people driving strategy mapping and implementation need a cross-silo framework for dealing with risk if they are to collaborate on overall risk management priorities
- Risk functions and digital functions could lead the way by demonstrably working hand in hand across organizational silos

5

As we came around the final bend, I was on the outside and my legs felt tired and heavy but I managed to find a hidden source of energy and "kick" some extra speed to overtake Seb Coe and get to the line first. A sweet victory.

Seb Coe was perhaps the best middle-distance runner in the world and had a mean "kick" off the final bend when he ran in the 800m and 1500m. He was an Olympic gold medallist of course (oh and he organized an Olympics once as well) and had some famous battles with other runners including Steve Ovett. I still remember their amazing battle(s) at the Moscow Olympics.

Being in the Boys' Brigade, I tended towards conservative, establishment figures so it was quite easy for me to back Seb instead of the wilder and more unpredictable Steve although in later years I found myself able to appreciate both in equal measure.

Although my favourite British athlete at that time was, of course, Alan Wells (100m/200m Scottish legend) I did sometimes find myself running the longer distances imagining myself being Seb Coe and hearing in my head the distinctive voice of David Coleman commentating on my "big kick off the last corner".

Some (few if any) might say it was always fated that Seb and I would meet in a head-to-head clash but perhaps an even smaller number would have predicted that it would be me who emerged victorious.

We were both in Zurich (which as Athletics fans will know hosts some big track and field events) one summer when I first caught a glimpse of him at the airport. He was the first track and field athlete I'd seen close up since I saw Tessa Sanderson stepping off a transfer bus at the opening ceremony of the Commonwealth games in Edinburgh in the late 80s. She waved at a few of us as we came out of the stadium after having completed our section performance at the opening ceremony - she was on her way in for the Athletes' parade and I remember she had a fabulously warm aura.

Speaking of opening ceremonies, I remember as a child staying up late watching (for several hours) the opening ceremony of the Olympics in Montreal. I was only little and kept dosing off so my Mum and Dad eventually asked 'why don't you go to bed, son?'

'I can't go to bed yet'
'Why not?'
'I want to see the pole vault'

Yes folks, I thought all the events followed the opening ceremony and took place on the same night and I really wished they would hurry up and get on with it!

I suppose I was only about five years old so can be excused that particular misunderstanding although it only goes to show that a little knowledge (that the pole vault would take place at the Olympics) can be a dangerous thing!

Such trauma was well and truly erased when I was lucky enough to attend the Opening Ceremony of the London Olympics in 2012. Like many fellow Brits, we feared the worst in terms of what the ceremony might contain and let's not forget the terrorism threat either. Emotions were high.

In the end, could there be anyone in the UK who wasn't absolutely bursting with pride at the magnificent show put on by Danny Boyle and the entire team? The whole thing was fantastic and when Mohammad Ali made his appearance the whole place went wild and all I could think of when there was nothing but (a lot of) space between me and the real-life incarnation of such a hero to millions, was my own dear Dad who was in a home with Alzheimer's and Parkinson's diseases but always agreed with so many that Ali was "the greatest"! And that moment when Steve Redgrave - the bookies' favourite to light the Olympic flame, instead handed the torch to the youths... oh man, I get goosebumps just thinking about it - even today.

Anyway, I digress. Let's get back to the race with me and Seb... before his London glory.

The flight from Zurich to London City airport went smoothly and we all departed and headed off (pull-along overnight cases in hand like relay batons) into the very small terminal building.

It was a moderate stretch to the end of the corridor before a right-hand corner into the passport hall and it was about half-way along the hall that I clocked that Seb Coe was in front of me - diagonally to my right.

As we approached the corner, I seized my chance and launched my "kick".

It worked like a dream. Seb had no time to react and before he knew it I crossed the line to be first to passport control where I proudly handed my passport to the immigration guard who looked for a minute like he might question the sweat on my brow but instead just waved me through. I knew not to wave to the crowd in that situation so settled for a self-congratulatory moment as I toddled off to make my way home.

So there we have it, good people, the moment I out-kicked Seb Coe on the last corner to cross the line first.

Of course, he might not have seen it like that.

In his mind, he was probably thinking something like "OMG there is so much to do in time for the London Olympics. Why did I agree to do this? If it all goes belly-up then I'll be the one to take all the blame. It was so much easier when all I had to do was run a race instead of the entire event. I wonder if... wait a minute, who is this idiot cutting in front of me? What a w...."

Or something like that.

Like my other celebrity encounters, there are probably quite a few risk management lessons that could be taken but here are a few of my selected tips.

Pick your battles

I spotted an opportunity to win by taking Seb Coe on the last bend and took it. I won that battle.

I've won many battles in my time. Whatever role I was in, there were battles to be fought - with competitors, within my own team and occasionally even with clients. Most of them were not easy battles to win and even if I was convinced I was right (and I sometimes was, though not always), we all know that being right is the easy bit. Bringing others around to your point of view is the difficult bit. Although on the face of it, I am typically mild mannered, deep down I know I am a bit of a scrapper. When I want something enough, I can be very single-minded in trying to get it. I remember an old boss of mine from Willis stating I was single-minded in my annual review and I got all upset because I didn't really know what it meant at the time (I thought it was similar to narrow minded) so did not realise he meant it as a compliment.

It was nevertheless an indicator of my determination and sometimes forcefulness of character even at the early stages of my career. I remember an occasion when I was about 12 months (yes months, not years) into my career and telling someone in an open meeting that what they were proposing for graduates was "wrong". For someone who could be very tactful at times, there were occasions when the red mist descended and before I knew it I had said something which with the benefit of hindsight, only had the effect of winding someone up the wrong way. I was probably right in whatever it was I happened to be arguing for but telling someone they are "wrong" is a red flag for diplomacy isn't it?

And if you wind up someone who happened to be at the front of the queue when God gave out influence and aggression then you need to take cover pretty quickly and consider whether that was a battle worth fighting or not.

Personal risk management of this nature also applies in more explicit conversations about risk. One of the main challenges for risk professionals is often getting others to do things in a different way. Now there are lots of behavioural change techniques open to people but leaving them aside for now, we can all envisage the sorts of characters that risk specialists come up against.

Firstly, there is the "yes, I'll do it" person. There are two different types of character here - one who really means they will do it and one who has no intention of keeping their word.

Secondly, there is the "I haven't got time for this" person. Again, there are two different types of character here - one who understands what he should do but genuinely just hasn't got time to do it, and one who says this to sound important or busy but in fact does not understand enough about what you are saying to properly build it into his thinking about priorities.

I'm simplifying things of course but risk management progress can be hampered by individuals displaying features of these different caricatures.

Anyway, this tip is all about picking your battles. There will be those who say it shouldn't be a 'battle'. They might point out that the logic for what they are proposing means that the answer is obvious (which assumes everyone follows logic which we know they can't always be relied to do in a work environment!). Alternatively, they might point out that we "are all in this together... all on the same side" so using a word like 'battle' gives the wrong impression. Watch out for folk like that - they could be utopian ideologists or worse, passive-aggressives. Neither can be fully trusted.

Of course there are battles! Tensions exist in all organisations for a whole multitude of reasons and so battles take place all the time. Some might be big battles but most are smaller and more micro in nature but they are still battles to be won or lost or, very occasionally, tied.

We just need to pick them very carefully if we want to make a positive difference.

The trouble is, when you are dealing with risk issues, it's not always possible just to sit back and do nothing for now... waiting for a different battle on another day. Some risk developments and issues are so important that they need to be raised and a conversation ("battle") is required today. After all, the stakes can be high for those involved. Heads of Risk experience tension like this fairly frequently - especially those in industries with strong and potentially intrusive regulators who will go after the Head of Risk as well as the CEO and others in the C-suite if they are not happy.

For those people (and let's remember, like you and me they are human beings too) the question to oneself of "Is this a battle I want to have today?" needs to be followed up with "Do I still need to have it anyway?" and it is this second question that some will say is not asked often enough... which is why we don't see the rate of progress in risk management in some organisations that we might otherwise witness.

To a learner of English, "He's a survivor" sounds like a compliment but whenever I've heard it levied at someone, it's usually derogatory in nature - implying that the person has not had the battles he arguably should have done.

Maybe those sorts of people are masters at picking their battles so maybe there is something we can learn from them. Maybe we could all learn to be like them - you know, sycophantic. In some industries and career choices, it's certainly common place to be like this.

When it comes to risk management, there are moments when sycophantic behaviour probably is appropriate but my point is that if there is too much of it then we won't get anywhere on dealing with thorny risk issues and uncertainty.

If we can't challenge people on their management of risk then where would that leave us? In lands of unknown depths of riskiness - that's where.

I wonder if there are organisations where challenge is welcome throughout the business except in relation to risk management. Imagine that one. "We have a culture of challenge and continuous improvement" would be a headline corporate value and admirable one too but the small print underneath it would say "except in relation to risk issues because we don't like to be challenged on the true levels of risk we are taking and the true effectiveness and/or efficiency of our risk management efforts."

I think there are probably some organisations which could be much healthier if there was more effective dialogue and challenge on risk related matters. The CEO and the Head of Risk (Chief Risk Officer) need to work together to bring that about, of course as in all but the smallest organisations, I don't think one can do it without the other given the current state of risk management capability in most organisations. In fact, the more you think about it, the more you can see that good collaboration between the CEO and CRO could result in both being smarter about the battles they do have (and with who) on risk.

I can imagine that Seb Coe had a "battle or two" including several on risk issues when he was organising the London Olympics. I bet he used his old mantras about there being other battles on other days a few times. I also bet he picked his battles with great skill.

Maybe we should all be skilful in picking our battles... or at least consider whether we wish to battle before we jump into one.

Of all the battles I've had in my time, the race against Seb Coe is maybe one of the most meaningless and definitely one I didn't think about very hard before I launched myself into it. However, the memory of it has outlived so many of the others which I did think more carefully about and which would not make such an interesting tale to tell years afterwards. I mean, what if I hadn't chosen to race Seb Coe around that last corner into passport control? What kind of story would that have been? Loser.

Enjoy your successes

I didn't do a lap of honour when I beat Seb to passport control. I didn't jump in the air with celebration or collapse exhausted onto the ground with my arms outstretched in glory in the way that he used to. Oh no, I'm far too big a man to stoop to that type of public celebration.

Did I celebrate it at all? No... not until I wrote this book. In fact, I'm not sure I've told anyone about the race until now. That's the sort of humble victor I am.

Let's leave my reasons for that aside though and flip into the world of risk management.

Risk never stops... it always carries on. Yes, individual risks might be controlled or avoided in some way but at an overall level there is always risk in an organization and/or initiative and in my experience its often just above the level which feels comfortable.

Whether I am in the "first line" i.e. with direct responsibility for risk or in the "second line" helping/advising others manage risk there is always something to worry about. It never ends.

Now as my wife will tell you, I like nothing better than a good worry! If Seb Coe and his committee had decided to introduce "worrying" as a demonstration event at the Olympics, I'd have been the favourite for the gold medal - having established my fretting credentials though the regional and national championships before sailing through the qualifying rounds at the "Worrylympics" and securing my place in the big final.

On Super Saturday in the Olympic stadium in East London, with the exuberant and continually expectant crowd clapping all around me like they do for long jumpers I'd have stepped up, gingerly, to the white line with one of the greatest expressions of worry the world has ever seen and blown away the competition - themselves highly respected and revered worriers from all around the globe.

Although not sure if it was allowed by the harassed looking officials, I would then have rewarded the roaring crowd with a triple high five with Jessica Ennis-Hill, Mo Farah and Greg Rutherford.

Weeks afterwards, I'd probably have entered into a broadcasting deal with Alan Richardson to co-present his "Ultimate Worrier" program.

Alas, worrying was not introduced at the Olympics and so Great Britain and Northern Ireland was denied another gold.

I don't actually worry *all* the time. It's actually not good for you to do so - it'll drive you crazy - but rest assured that when I am in the worry zone, I am truly world class at it.

For those involved in risk, it is good to have the right level of worry about the uncertainty and risk which lies ahead. It's good to be able to say "I'm on it" when other stakeholders expect you to be exhibiting the right level of worry and consequent action.

The thing is, as well as worrying well, it is important to enjoy your successes too. It's too easy to rush on to worrying about the next thing and miss the opportunity to feel good and make others feel good about what you have just achieved.

When you next have a success of whatever scale and magnitude, just take a moment to think about what's just happened. Look at the good that has just occurred. Enjoy the sensation and allow your team to enjoy it too.

You probably won't enjoy it too much because you or other worriers will exercise a degree of calibration on that but there is a chance you will miss the endorphin release so make sure you take the opportunity to feel good and even great about your success.

Of course, some successes can be enjoyed forever. Seb Coe can forever enjoy many things including his come-back against Steve Ovett for his successful shot at gold, second time around, in Moscow. For me, my career success to be enjoyed forever was coming up through the ranks to be made full equity Partner at EY.

Great coaches will tell you that is possible to evoke the feeling of past success by touching something. In short what you do, is think about something you achieved in the past which was really great for you. You think about how great it made you feel physically and mentally and while you are doing that you touch a part of your body like your arm or something. For example, you might touch your wedding ring or place one hand over the other clenched fist etc. What happens is that you then associate that touching with the feeling so that it becomes possible to release the feeling simply by touching.

I know it sounds weird.

I was a bit sceptical when I tried it once with a wonderful coach of mine and do you know, it bloomin' worked! To this day, I am able to feel great about a past work achievement simply by touching one hand onto another in a certain way.

I was so impressed that I used a different association for two other situations. One is where I need to be very brave (I mean in a life-risking way) and another is where I need to "let go" emotionally about something because there is nothing I can do about it.

I'll spare you the details on those but both are anchored in past events and I have the ability to bring on the emotional mental/physical feeling at will.

Anyway, I'm digressing again dear reader and you are supposed to not let me do that. Shame on you.

Where were we? Ah yes, some successes last forever in memories and some can be fleeting - passing moments which will be forgotten about by Thursday morning never mind eternity.

Just enjoy them. You work hard enough to achieve them and everyone has their fair share of sad to deal with so don't deny yourself the opportunity to celebrate and be happy when you've earned it.

Remember that what seems like a battle and a success to you might not even have been noticed by the other party

...so keep context in mind before you go around boasting about it too much!

I love the thought that Seb Coe might one day hear of this encounter of which he will currently be entirely oblivious. I love even more that his likely reaction if he did ever hear of it would be to shrug it off as the nonsense it is and move on to more important matters like where is the buffet.

This serves as quite a useful example of something to keep in mind - what seems like a battle to you might not even register as anything like that to the other party.

This enables you to be confident. If you assume that the other person doesn't think of the situation as a battle then you can be more assured that what you are seeking is maybe not such a big ask after all.

However, the flip side is that you might end up celebrating something which isn't, how can I say, worthy of it.

Maybe you didn't set your bar high enough? Maybe if you had asked for more it would have felt more like a battle?

Hmm... maybe I am just worrying too much and/or stretching too far for a third lesson from this encounter.

It just seems to me that if you are likely to be using risk management case studies in your organization then it's important to make sure they resonate properly with all those involved. For example, of your organizational governance is under scrutiny and you are trying to use case studies to demonstrate its efficacy then it's important to make sure they stand up.

Claiming that you challenged others and had a healthy exchange of views about things before they decided to do their own thing anyway only stacks up if the other party feels that it was indeed a robust encounter.

Another example would be claiming to have had an impact in a Board meeting because there was a risk item listed for consideration just before A.O.B. Before you say anything, I know that best practice is to have risk considerations threaded through Board meeting rather than as a separate item only. That's not the point I'm trying to make here though. I'm saying that to an extent, it's the other party's context which values the success you've just had.

Okay, my little one-sided story of a battle with Seb Coe is entertaining and allowed me to introduce some broader risk management lessons but at the same time it enables me to make the point that from his perspective it meant nothing at all.

Maybe one day I will be in a battle with Seb Coe. That might seem unlikely unless he releases a book about the same time as I release this one. I probably won't ever get the chance to do proper battle with him but I might just get the chance to do proper battle with people on who's radars I have not registered to date.

Maybe it will be the same for you. Who might you have liaised with in your organization who wouldn't yet consider that they'd had a proper "battle" with you?

By the way, don't be angry and go all aggressive into fights - that's definitely not what I'm recommending - even if it sometimes seems it is the only way in some organisations!

If you want to make change happen though and bring about risk management improvement then there might just be some difficult conversations to be had and some tense moments to be navigated (rather than circumvented). You will be on the radar and you will be having battles if you are adding value in risk.

Go bravely, dear traveller.

6

BIG BROTHER HAS A COUSIN – Keeping an eye on edge
technology in the Internet of Things and People

LinkedIn article:

Warning: If you don't like creative analogies then don't read
this. Okay, well don't say I didn't warn you!

Hi everybody. Like many futurologists... and businessmen...
George Orwell got the timing wrong. For George, it was
with his dystopian vision of "1984". Thankfully, at least so
far, much of the imagined future world turned out to be
wrong as well as the timing although some of it is arguably
appearing on the horizon. Maybe all George was doing was
planting some warnings. That's serious stuff for humanity
and I'm not going to do those arguments justice in a short
article like this one.

Instead, I'm going to talk about a relative because Big
Brother has a cousin.

Big Brother's cousin

He is an interesting cousin and not to be ignored. He's
exciting with some very attractive features but for some
people, some of the time, he is a worry.

He is not interested in constant surveillance by the
authorities in the way that the elusive Big Brother was. He is
a very keen and detailed observer, though.

He is less interested in what the ruling parties want and more
interested in what the majority of people want.

Sounds like a more reasonable chap and he, or she, could
well be but there are some things to watch out for, aren't

there?

---

*'Some people lose out as big
swinging algorithms swagger down
Big Data Boulevard'*

Big Brother's cousin is mainly interested in "most"

People ask who Big Brother's cousin is and indeed whether
he actually exists at all. For example, what if he is a
machine? What if he is an artificially intelligent machine –
one who can work out what most people want and give it to
them in a way which seems almost automatic? If he is, then I
wonder who built him and how the programming could get
so sophisticated that it could work all that out and link to
objects in peoples' houses to deliver what they want... there
and then. When I say 'what they want', I mean 'what most
people like them would want' in those circumstances. It's
not guaranteed that any particular individual truly wants
what they end up getting from Big Brother's cousin. Some
people lose out as big swinging algorithms swagger down
Big Data Boulevard.

Challenge for Big Brother's cousin

Whoever feeds Big Brother's cousin (whether it be feeding
rice or data, or both) has got a couple of important things to
think about, hasn't he/she/it? The Internet of Things and
People (because we must never forget their fundamental
roles in the whole thing) throws up some challenges for Big
Brother's cousin including:

1)   Accident of desires: Focusing on what most people
want can miss what some people want/need. Minority
desires can sometimes be served by Big Brother's cousin but
only if there is money in it. For you see, Big Brother's

cousin ruthlessly chases the masses

2)   Accident of discovery: Big Brother's cousin uses apparent correlations to serve the masses. He needs to be sure of them – the accuracy of the data and the reliability of its use. He needs to know the data is not corrupt and that the correlation will stand up to be true over time. For you see, Big Brother's cousin needs this competitive differentiator to survive if he is to operate honestly

3)   Accident of birth: What about peoples' needs that are not as a result of choice but accident of birth and through that accident of birth they are in a 'forgotten minority'? For you see, Big Brother's cousin is not a charity

Wow – Big Brother's cousin must be very busy dealing with all this… or at least he would be if he existed, which he doesn't. Well, not so far as I am aware, anyway unless he was somehow a collection of things thing that...

Still with me? No?... well just run with it for now, please.

Who is Big Brother's cousin, then?

Wait a minute, if Big Brother's cousin doesn't actually exist then who is doing all this stuff? Who is fuelling demand for these internet services and operating them but also caring about how they should operate? I think the answer is (and go along with me on this because otherwise the article doesn't work) that we are all, collectively, Big Brother's cousin… we all play different parts in feeding, supporting, maintaining and using the Internet of Things and People whether in our private lives or through the organizations we work for.

'...we are all, collectively, Big

Brother's cousin'

At a very personal level, we share our data online very openly – sometimes because we believe it will help us get what we want more easily. We go along with automated "majority steers" because they are typically accurate in reflecting our needs.

When we think about it, we also appreciate that we sometimes share information by mistake which can stop us getting what we want. We are also capable of realising that the influence of majority routes can steer us away from what is truly valuable to us.

We can see the potential upside and the potential downside so we all need to work on getting the balance right as Big Brother's cousin (who is only an infant) takes his future form at an increasingly rapid pace.

Ethical decisions for Big Brother's cousin

At a deeper level it is fascinating for some, exciting for some and worrying for some to consider the more ethical aspects of Big Brother's cousin.

For example, decisions need to be made about whether living in a storm-prone area is more worthy of general support from the rest of the population (for example, via subsidised insurance) than being born with a genetic condition which might influence life expectancy. Come to think of it, is a bad driver who thinks he is good more worthy of subsidised insurance safety nets than these other two examples? The Internet of Things and People will influence decisions of that nature.

These topics are more complex to work through and resolve than I can go into here but they are example areas of ethical decision making which were made in the past – perhaps in silos and without the information increasingly becoming available nowadays which makes it more possible to be selective… perhaps to the benefit of the many and the detriment of the few (which may or may not be a good thing if you want to get philosophical - as indeed we might need to). Utilitarians at the ready!

'...drawing new lines for people to be on the wrong side of'

Sharper products and services but they might not suite you

Many of you will know how it feels to be on the wrong side of a decision "not to do something anymore because it is not economic". It is frustrating to hear that "the route wasn't profitable", "we don't want your 'difficult' insurance business anymore", "we've changed the range and your product line is discontinued" and I'm pretty sure it is becoming more common.

As people in organizations become better informed and are programing robots to be smarter, we will continue to see sharpening of products and services - drawing new lines for people to be on the wrong side of. Big Brother's cousin will need to think about the three accidents we discussed earlier, and other important things too, as progress gets made and the ethical aspects of such decisions come into stark focus.

'Big Brother's cousin likes very big data and he knows more about you than you think'

Edge technology

The development of edge technology, where the focus is on how and how fast the right decentralised decisions are made by technology using data at the point (the 'edge') of interaction with the customer is a particular area where the implications of our changing world will manifest themselves. 'Getting it right' at the edge has implications for strategic risk management and compliance as well as customer satisfaction and organizational gain. The film "Robocop" seems a stretch in this article but when you think about it, as I'm sure you will, it provides analogous examples of how edge technology might influence things both intentionally and by "accident".

Of course, getting it right also means accessing all available information that might be useful to the interaction – not like the old days of you keying it in or your computer asking if you wanted to autofill. While most of us are probably okay with the prospect of Amazon recommending coffee pods because we bought a coffee machine (let's call that 'big data'), the possible implications of something we might call 'very big data' are at a whole new level. Big Brother's cousin likes very big data and he knows more about you than you think.

Conclusion

As greater advances are made in edge technology, it will be important to ensure that proper consideration is given to the way in which decentralised decisions will shape the Internet of Things and People. Some of those decisions can be big ones with very significant ethical dimensions and implications for people and so it seems sensible to do a good job of this. That means that we need to ensure that every decision (at the edge or otherwise) is structured and made with proper consideration of the risk and uncertainty associated with the opportunity. Big Brother's cousin is a focal point for this activity and could be a great ally to us.

> We all have a stake in ensuring the future is truly what we want it to be. Collectively, we have the power.

At the time I set out to write this article, I felt I could see things pretty clearly. I'd had a very enjoyable but busy few months since leaving EY and increasingly it seemed to me like I was increasingly gaining a line of sight on things that I hadn't had for a long time.

Three things caught my attention at the time: Big (very big) data, and its onwards march; Popularism, and the nasty effect that being mostly interested in the majority can sometimes have on the good of the whole and; Big swinging algorithms (the power that was being given to them and those who owned them) and yes the 'big swinging...' bit was a direct reference to investment banking troubles (or joy, depending on your point of view) of the past. Of course, "Big Data Boulevard" was one of my alliterative originals!

The first two of these three things were getting quite a lot of media coverage at the time. One aspect of the third one was too - the power of those who owned the algorithms was a fascinating journey in business theory for many involved but the power being given to the algorithms themselves was receiving less attention.

I had these things all running around in my head with the feeling that there were some strong risk management considerations to these aspects.

I was worried and those who know me will tell you that such a mental state is not unusual for me.

Let me clarify something, though. I wasn't worried about the subjects themselves as there can be a lot of good in these drivers of our future. What I was more worried about at the time was whether the risks associated with pursuing the opportunities would be managed well.

Keep in mind that many people would argue there was still a general deficiency in risk management education (and capability) in C-suites and management and workforce across the board. I know that such a statement would be a sweeping generalization but it's a feeling I've been used to ever since I did my degree in risk management in the late 80s and joined the world's workplace only to realise that I knew more about risk management than nearly everyone else. I don't mean that I knew more than others about managing individuals risks in particular situations in specific companies in all industries etc. That's not what I'm saying. I'm saying that when it comes to understanding the opportunity available to manage risk in a structured way across enterprises, there was (and still is) a long way to go.

But let's not get stuck on that.

Let's just say that I had the feeling risk professionals would not be all over these three big developments in our world at a time when I thought it would be more important than ever for them to be close to the action.

I was looking for a central theme to hang these thoughts from by way of an article and I think it was mid-way through one of the older versions of George Orwell's 1984 on the telly (never as good as the book, I know) when it struck me that the "ever-watching" overlord could catch people's attention.

Only it wouldn't be Big Brother himself as he already had a whole set of hallmarks assigned to him. So, I went for his cousin and started to think about how I would describe him in the article (which I did).

It wasn't quite as eye-catching as "The Devil's Wife" which was the title a couple of old friends used for a piece of music they wrote many decades ago but I was quite pleased with it!

Of course, as the article developed I drew the conclusion that Big Brother's cousin is actually all of us collectively. We can decide how we operate to take advantage of the opportunities ahead but in a socially responsible way.

I'm still not sure if I fully believe that we actually do have the collective ability to change things anymore. Increasing wealth disparity means I sometimes struggle to convince myself of that but I am ever hopeful that we do and will continue to have it.

I made the point about people being at the heart of things because I believe they always are. It's easy to forget that The Internet of Things is created, operated and used by people... at least for now. With risk goggles on, that means that the management of risk in the IoT will be underpinned by people risk, which elsewhere I have explained as underpinning all other risk management activity. Or put another way, people risk undermines all other risks.

The "accidents" I came up with - Desires, Discovery and Birth - were challenges that I could see needed to be addressed and were actually hooks on which pro-active risk professionals could use to at least bring some focus to their involvement.

It's easy to think everything is fine when you are on the "right side" of the lines drawn by Big Brother's cousin. It's only when you find yourself on the "wrong side" that you begin to worry and worry, I did.

I chose to draw attention to the use of AI in edge technology as this was where I felt people were walking (I hoped not sleep-walking) into the unknown and should therefore in theory be a place where established ways of operating had not yet been fully set so there was opportunity to have risk considered in a better way to support those activities.

If you are not sure what edge technology means, I can tell you it is a lot simpler than it sounds.

I like to think of it as the interface points between the organisation and its customers (although it can also be suppliers and other stakeholders etc). It is the place where business touches the customer. In particular, it's where an app or some other type of IT represents the organization at that point in time and is the mechanisms through with the organisation liaises with its customers (or other stakeholders). There are lots of different edges even inside the same organization because they communicate with their customers in different ways about different things but the important point is that a computer is making decisions (following its programming, by a human) and directly relaying them to the customer without further reference to the corporate centre.

My point was the three accidents were all challenges to be addressed in programming those "edge" interactions and that therefore organisations would want to address the ethical considerations and other risks at the time the edge was designed (and subsequently monitored).

I thought that in-house risk functions should want to be all over this and that it could be a great opportunity to craft the right approach to managing risk in these situations.

For such a big issue, I was really disappointed with the readership and responses I - er, didn't get. I thought the article would provoke some good discussion and was really pleased with two early contributors including an ex colleague from EY (for some reason, it's rare for people inside EY to like content published from people who have left EY) and so was quite optimistic about follow up comments and likes. Sadly, they never came.

61

Maybe I published it at the wrong time of the week. Maybe people don't like anything to do with Big Brother. Maybe people just switched off at the beginning liked I asked them to do if they didn't like creative analogies. Maybe the LinkedIn algorithm didn't like conversations about algorithms! Anyway, it didn't fly and I think I only got about 100 views of it in the end. The topic seems as important as ever though.

Nearly three years later, I participated in an online event where they ran a poll to gauge involvement in this sort of thing. Although in no way could it be considered a statistically significant sample, it was disappointing that the majority of risk functions were not close to the action and I wonder now if that opportunity has gone for good (except in an independent review type capacity)?

At the time of writing this book, the UK was thrown into school exam chaos because of the use of algorithms to predict grades for exams which had been cancelled due to the virus. Although there have already been some government u-turns, and the full truth is still to emerge, it looks like the only reliable thing about the algorithms were that they could be blamed for the, some would say, scandal. It looks like people from poorer backgrounds have been adversely selected against by the algorithm or let's be clearer about it, those who programmed the algorithm and those who used it.

I think the main risk management lessons from this article are:
1) Technology brings fabulous new ways of operating but we need to put an ethical hat on when it comes to how it could/should operate
2) We need to ensure that every decision (at the edge or otherwise) is structured and made with proper consideration of the risk and uncertainty associated with the opportunity
3) Risk functions should be able to add value to the consideration of risk on the edge

4) People risk undermines the Internet of Things so needs to be managed appropriately
5) Maybe (but only maybe) we collectively have the power to shape how AI in edge technology and the IoT will be

7

FORMULA ONE

LinkedIn article:

What has Formula 1 ever done for Risk Management?

Fans of Monty Python might immediately think this article is a nod to the "What have the Romans ever done for us?" sketch but it isn't. No mention will be made of that. None whatsoever.

Fans of motor safety will have a long list of safety devices in everyday car usage which emanated from Formula 1 research and development. I'm not talking about that either although it is clearly a risk management contribution made and one which has no doubt saved many lives.

This article is about neither of those. Instead, it's far more personal but with broad applicability.

Clients of mine from the time (about five or so years ago) will remember me using Formula 1 as an analogy to describe the new risk management effectiveness framework I had developed while at EY. They might even recall me relaying my excitement when David Coulthard said during a television race commentary that "Formula 1 is the ultimate form of risk management". I don't know if he was right but given I was using the F1 analogy at the time it was a fabulous boost to morale!

Anyway, my aim was to simplify and my thinking was as follows.

There were only three things to think about in terms of

effectiveness in F1:

1. THE KIT: not just the car but all the equipment (hardware and software) in the pits and of course back at base
2. THE PEOPLE: not just the driver but the pit lane crew and all the people back at base
3. THE SETUP FOR ANY PARTICULAR RACE TRACK: Monte Carlo needs a very different setup than Monza

Each of these three areas could have specific evaluation and assessment criteria (as well as lots of granular assessment items). For example, you could assess PEOPLE individually but their ability to work together effectively was also a worthy assessment to make in terms of overall effectiveness. The same too for the KIT... it wasn't just about the effectiveness of the individual components but about the extent to which they operated in a seamless fashion.

I didn't know anything much about the detail of these three items and I didn't claim to know much at all about F1 – except that I enjoyed watching it and harboured dreams of being an F1 driver every time I got behind the wheel of a go-kart!

Could those three things to think about in F1 also be the same three things to think about when it came to assessing the effectiveness of risk management in business? Well, we hadn't thought that way in the past. We had more than three categories we used for risk management effectiveness assessments then. Sometimes we used risk categories, sometimes we used other categorizations but always more than three. Forget the past though, could it work? After all, it would make things simpler and easier for others to understand.

Well, the KIT would be the risk management framework

components – policies, procedures, systems, models etc.

The PEOPLE would be all those involved in managing risk, formally or informally, in different departments and also through committees. External influencers such as regulators and investors would also play their part.

The SETUP would be the way in which the KIT is applied by the PEOPLE to the underlying business processes of the organization. For example, the use of risk management techniques when setting strategy will be different from their use when executing strategy. Another example would be in an insurance company, where the way in which risk management systems and processes are adapted for underwriting will be different from claims even though there will be similarities and an underlying consistency. In the same way, the set-up for one business might not be right for another… they might need the same things but set-up differently.

We put more granular handles on all three dimensions in terms of what is assessed and how it can be evaluated. Granular handles are important for being able to arrive at priority actions, aren't they? We found a place for all the previous effectiveness assessment criteria we had used under the three dimensions which meant we could use the F1 analogy in training after all!

On the point about evaluation, it wasn't just about outcomes. The best driver and the best car don't always win every race in F1. Stuff happens on a personal level as well as on a technical level so while outcomes might be a good long-term retrospective indicator of effectiveness they don't in themselves provide the complete picture needed to understand effectiveness, today and how to improve the chances of winning today's race.

I found the F1 analogy particularly helpful when training people in risk management and helping them to get their head around all the different things which influence risk management effectiveness and I hope you will find a use for it too. Fans of motorsport or not, the analogy helped people understand.

So thank you David Coulthard, thank you F1 and thank you to those at EY who helped me develop the risk management effectiveness framework at that time! Time has passed, people and things have moved on but the analogy still works and the need to explain things in a simple way so that others understand and can do something with it is as great as ever.

Of all the risk management related subjects I've spoken to organisations about, understanding its effectiveness is the one where the responses have been least convincing.

That's not to say that risk management always needs to be fully effective because it doesn't need to be. Rather, it's level of effectiveness should be understood so that key stakeholders can be confident it is where they think it is.

Although I had thought about this before, Solvency II (which prompted lots of aligned regulation around the management of risk in insurance companies) brought the effectiveness into sharp focus for me but not for many others.

The reason for the disconnect was that the Solvency II guidance listed out lots of things that firms needed to have in place. A "level 1" requirement was to have a Risk Management System which was effective so a nice clear statement there you might think.

However, it went on to list a multitude of other things at "level 2". There was not too much wrong with those level 2 requirements which listed things like risk policies, risk governance arrangements, risk appetite statements, and the need for control assessments etc.

The problem was that because level 2 was a long list of things, many firms believed that if they did everything listed at level 2, it would mean that everything at level 1 would automatically be covered - which is wasn't. Most of the items listed in level 2 were tangible things that you could read/use/point to etc. Whilst the effectiveness of those items in terms of design could be assessed, there was little else with which to gauge effectiveness.

So how could I make this easier to understand?

It seemed to me that using the Formula 1 analogy again would be a good thing to do as I'd be able to help people understand that the "KIT" alone doesn't win any races so why should that be the only thing which gets attention in risk management effectiveness reviews in insurance companies or elsewhere?

It also helped make points about individual versus collective PEOPLE performance and also that risk management capability needed to be tuned into specific parts of the organization instead of applied in the same way on every occasion.

In real life, people have always seemed to like this analogy (whether they are motor racing fans or not). I think they like it because it is easy to grasp the concepts. It's actually more difficult to apply it in practice though because of the interplays between the different dimensions etc but the really useful thing about this way of thinking is the way in which handles can be attached to different components so that assessments of effectiveness and associated improvements can actually be very precise and specific which makes progress (and improved contribution) easier to measure... even if it is on a relative basis.

While they might like the analogy, the problem with pointing out all the things that people have missed is that it doesn't always come as good news.

Not only that, but if they do undertake more work to properly understand effectiveness, it might lead to them having to do more improvement work and what would that lead to, eh?

Over time, many firms began to grasp the concept of effectiveness though and whether they followed my approach or developed their own, many assertions were made about risk management effectiveness along the lines of "our system of risk management and internal control is fully effective". Although the intentions are commendable, I've never trusted such statements because risk is unpredictable and so are people. It's always felt more honest to me if a firm says something like "this is how we have improved risk management effectiveness over the past year and this is how we intend to continue doing so into the future" etc. That sort of (more relative than absolute) statement can also lead to a far richer dialogue about priorities.

Anyway, many organisations got themselves comfortable that their risk management systems were as effective as they needed to be.

If we assume for a minute that they were correct then what that meant was that as at the time of the assessment, things were good.

As at the time the analysis took place, everything was where it should be... but then what? Time moves on so does effectiveness remain where it should be as the world around it changes?

It was with this temporal challenge in mind that I wrote the follow-up article.

LinkedIn article:

Vroom Vroom: Formula 1 Risk Management Effectiveness has just changed - how about yours?

I wonder what Formula 1 teams have done about risk management effectiveness between race seasons this year... what do you reckon? I wonder what we can learn from their attitude and approach.

Fans of my analogy on this will remember the LinkedIn article where we considered effectiveness within and between three main aspects;

1. THE KIT
2. THE PEOPLE
3. THE SETUP FOR ANY PARTICULAR RACETRACK.

You might even remember how we thought this was also a good way to structure assessment of risk management effectiveness in other businesses too (the link to the previous article is below).

Well, I don't know for sure what Formula 1 teams have done this year... you can't tell from the public coverage or the testing failures/successes or race results alone. As with other organisations, there are always economic limits to what can be spent but I'm pretty sure they will have assessed and improved the effectiveness of the KIT (the car and all the supporting technology) in terms of managing risk. Even if it is impossible to assess effectiveness in absolute terms, I'm pretty sure they will have evaluated things in relative terms. I'm also quietly confident that they won't simply have done this component by component in isolation. I am almost certain they will have looked at the linkages between the different components of the kit and made assessments and improvements in relation to that too.

70

I also guarantee you that PEOPLE risk management effectiveness improvements will have been made as well – not just drivers getting fitter and engineers becoming more knowledgeable – aspects of teaming between all those involved at the race tracks and back at HQ and in the supply chains will have been considered and improved too.

...changes will have been made in the pursuit of success and glory

The SETUPs will also be revisited this year. Things change – some of which are in the control of the teams (like many aspects of car design) and some of which are outside of their control (like racetrack layout changes and tyre rubber compounds). Changes have happened though so the SETUPs will be changed to improve risk management effectiveness for each race this time around.

The interaction between the three main aspects will also have been considered and most likely changes will have been made in pursuit of success and glory.

All of the teams will have done this subject to economic constraints and in recognition that risks will always remain. They will have been relentless in trying to optimize risk management effectiveness (whatever they call it and whatever terms they use) in their exciting world.

…for there is no room for complacency in relation to risk management in Formula 1. I can't imagine complacency being tolerated in those teams. No way. It would take a brave soul to suggest that optimized risk management last season means there is no need for changes this time around!

I wonder how this form of continuous risk management effectiveness improvement would compare to other businesses?

*...for there is no room for
complacency in relation to risk
management in Formula 1*

Situations will be different by organization and industry – of
course they will. Geography and culture will also play a part
as will regulatory requirements and the size and complexity
of the organization. Ambition and hunger will play their
parts too in terms of how well risk management
effectiveness has been assessed and improved.

Will we have seen the systematic consideration of
effectiveness within and between the three main aspects,
though? I'm not so sure. I don't think all organizations look
at risk management effectiveness in such a logically obvious
(but at the same time sophisticated) way.

*It would take a brave soul to suggest
that optimised risk management last
season means there is no need for
change this time around*

Yes, we will have seen improvements in individual
components in just about all organizations – whether or not
such improvements can be described cohesively from Head
Office. Some improvement will have been made in most
organizations, I'm sure – even if the improvement can only
be explained in local and relative terms rather than in
holistic and absolute terms.

72

There will have been progress and that is good.

Could it have been better, though? Maybe. Whatever happens in Formula 1 races this year, I'm pretty sure the teams will be able to say at the end of the season that they did their very best to manage risk effectively – it seems in their nature to drive (no pun intended) themselves and each other to do everything possible for strategic success.

I'd like to think that other organisations will also be able to state confidently that they did everything they could to optimize risk management effectiveness at the chequered flag of their business periods - why wouldn't they? Having clarity on what has been done and what is planned in relation to effectiveness within and between the three main aspects of effectiveness seems a good way to.

Vroom Vroom!

When I wrote this follow up article, I was really trying to make sure that complacency didn't set in on risk management effectiveness.

I'll be honest, I thought that I could use the glamour and excitement of Formula 1 again to draw attention to effectiveness which I was pretty sure still wasn't getting the attention it logically should. However, I realized I could do this via a slightly different route which was to draw out the fact that things change from one period to another.

My logic was that if people saw that Formula 1 teams never rest on their laurels in relation to managing risk then firms in often less glamorous but also often more complex industries shouldn't do so either. If people could see that success is only gained in Formula 1 by continually reassessing risk and uncertainty and risk management effectiveness and making the improvements to be better than your competitors, then they would realise the importance of doing the same.

Of course, in Formula 1, it is everything which is continually assessed... absolutely everything albeit in a proportionate way. In many non-motor racing firms, it was only the "KIT" which was being assessed and even then, often only some of it.

More generally, there was still some apprehension about making effort to uncover stuff which requires more effort to improve and might not represent such a direct and tangible link to winning as they do in Formula 1.

A couple of years on, where are we now when it comes to addressing the effectiveness of risk management?

Well I was sure it still varied a lot between firms and my work with The Risk Coalition's excellent initiative to produce guidance for Board Risk Committees and Risk Functions based on a very wide consultation process confirmed this. For some organisations, effectiveness assessments are very directly tied to detailed assessments of compliance with specific regulations put in place for particular risks and while they might provide useful information on those specific areas, it feels like broader effectiveness remains a relatively undeveloped area.

For other firms, the concept remains alien.

Not every racing team can even play at Formula 1 level though, let alone win so maybe we should not expect them to understand the way in which risk is managed at that level.

Perhaps the same is true in other organisations. Maybe only the best will have the best approach to managing risk which of course means taking risk well. I mean, if everybody did it, where would that leave us? Organisations continually improving to make well-informed decisions about good risk taking? It doesn't bear thinking about, does it?

From these two Formula 1 articles I think the main risk management tips are:

- If Formula 1 teams are never complacent about their ongoing risk management effectiveness, why should other commercial enterprises be?
- Risk management effectiveness can be better understood if you think in terms on KIT, PEOPLE and the SETUP for a particular situation
- Often, organisations think only of KIT when they address effectiveness
- An overall approach to understanding and improving risk management shouldn't be forgotten about when addressing the detail
- Beware generalized statements such as "risk management is fully effective"
- Even if it is impossible to accurately define and measure overall risk management effectiveness, relative progress can be easier to articulate and demonstrate

8

IMPROVING THE ABILITY OF INVESTORS TO
DIFFERENTIATE BETWEEN INVESTEES BASED ON RISK
MANAGEMENT EFFECTIVENESS DATA

LinkedIn article:

Imagine investors had full access to perfect information
on risk management effectiveness in investees. I wonder
what would happen.

They don't of course and perhaps it is unlikely that they
ever will have access to truly perfect information.

They might, however, get access to better information
than they currently do – risk management effectiveness
information which enables better differentiation between
investee firms.

Consider the sources of risk management effectiveness
information available to some/all investors at the
moment. They include:

• Published Reports & Accounts and other external
statements

• Credit ratings

• Past regulatory action

• Website information

• Past industry and individual company performance

• Statements made in meetings between firms and

76

investors

All of these, and other sources, shine light on certain aspects of risk management effectiveness, which underpin/undermine broader understanding of the riskiness of investees.

It sometimes seems as though at a high level within sectors, it is increasingly difficult to differentiate between firms based on the publicly available data. The same sorts of comments are made/disclosed on the same types of risks and issues.

Difficult-to-differentiate conclusions are drawn (where necessary to satisfy Financial Reporting Council standards etc) on things like the control environment (by which the firms usually mean the financial control environment which ensures accurate financial reporting rather than the broader control environment which probably has greater influence on future performance variability).

In due diligence situations, risk management effectiveness spotlights are only shone on areas which have typically always been reviewed in that type of exercise meaning that other aspects may not be addressed explicitly.

Spotlights shine light on particular aspects of risk management effectiveness but current practice seems to leave other aspects unlit to investors.

Where does that leave us?

One interpretation of current practice is that it leaves us with the potential to shine new light on aspects of risk management effectiveness which would support

> investors in differentiating between investees. I wonder who would want that?

In writing this article, it wasn't that I thought investors didn't have a view on the riskiness of those companies they invest in because I know that they do.

I was also aware that for some investors, their overall investment portfolio's riskiness is the main thing so there is less interest in individual companies' contribution to that portfolio as long as it doesn't change the overall shape of it too much.

I get both those dynamics.

It wasn't my intention to criticise investors for the interest in risk which they currently take and the analysis of risk which they continue to draw on for their input.

Neither was it my intention to imply any criticism of those companies who make a lot of effort to explain their risk management in external reports and make attestations required by supervisory bodies.

Right, that's that out of the way!

Let's adopt some future focus here and concentrate on how, going forward, things might be better for everyone. My own little question and answer session on this topic goes as follows:

- Could more risk management effectiveness information be provided to investors than currently is provided? Yes.
- Could it provide more confidence that the risk levels in the investee (and consequently in the portfolio) are at the levels currently believed? Yes.

- Could it enable differentiation between investee firms? Yes.
- Could that differentiating information be useful to investors and other stakeholders? Yes.
- How valuable would that information be? Er, not sure.

Sometimes it's quite hard to work out what the result would be if we did things in a different (and I'd argue better way) than is common practice and difficult to change.

My Q&A continues:
- Could it be done in most organisations? Yes.
- Is the know-how available to evaluate risk management effectiveness and efficiency? Yes.
- Who would push for it? Er, not sure.

Who pushes for change, eh? Who is brave enough and funded well enough to go for it? Who is smart enough to find a way to make it happen?

Ignoring past and current practice, the logic for a different way of operating still seems strong to me.

Maybe one day the aliens will arrive from another planet and after the initial pleasantries are exchanged and some intergalactic humour shared about the differences in our bodily functions, they'll get down to the serious stuff of asking why on earth (geddit?) we don't provide more transparent and differentiating data on risk management effectiveness in companies which are supposed to compete for our investments.

When we respond that it's because we've never done it that way before, they might well have a little chuckle.

That all assumes that the aliens have a sense of humour... and that they exist in the first place, or will exist in the future if we bring time travel into it!   Other scenarios are available, aren't they?

Anyway, visitors from other planets aside, I think the key tips from this chapter could be described as:

- It can be difficult to differentiate between companies based on publicly available risk management effectiveness data
- Beware generic statements made about risk management effectiveness in reports & accounts
- There is potential opportunity to shine new light on aspects of risk management effectiveness which would support investors in differentiating between investees
- It's not clear who would/should push for it

9

GEOFF HURST - "Some people are on the pitch, they think it's all over... it is now!"

The reason I was all alone with Geoff Hurst in a space no more than about 1 meter squared was to do with parking meters.

Before you start thinking we might have been bundled into the back of a police van because of a dispute about clamp release, let me reassure you that no crimes were committed that day... at least not by me or Geoff (as far as I am aware).

The truth is I was part of a team managing a tender process for a client and Geoff had arrived as part of one of the teams pitching for the work. He had arrived just in time and had been led up to the presentation room only to announce that he'd need to go out again to put more money in the parking meter. Ah yes, there were no mobile phone parking payment apps in those days. If you didn't have a ready supply of twenty pence pieces in your pocket then you'd have to move along even if you were an iconic, hat-trick scoring, World Cup winning England international football player!

The wonderful Willis office at Ten Trinity Square (which is now a lovely hotel) was a bit tricky to navigate so I was asked to "escort Mister Hurst" back down to the entrance to he could put more money in the meter. There was a secret "Chairman's lift" with capacity for only two people and I figured that Geoff was important enough to justify using it and that it would be a good route so in we went. I pressed the button for the ground floor, and we stood in silence watching the floor number lights.

Bong 2 - Bong 1 - Bong G.

"Here we are... now just through there, please."

A few moments later, we did the whole thing in reverse and went back into the room where the pitch was.

I was pretty sure that I had not given him any advantage over the other pitching teams that day. After all, I'd said virtually nothing. I also thought that maybe meeting megastar footballers and other celebrities was going to be commonplace in this line of business (it wasn't) so I should just keep my cool. Anyway, I was Scottish so it's not like he was Kenny Dalglish or anything, was it?

Blimey, for a bright kid, I was quite a numpty sometimes!

Did he and his team win the tender? I can't actually remember and I'm sure he didn't remember for very long either. After all, if you've been in a situation where winning means winning the football World Cup... not vicariously but by actually being on the pitch and physically winning it by thumping leather footballs into the back of the net, then I'm sure that other victories, however sweet at the time, don't make the cut when it comes to the career photo album!

My risk management tips from this encounter with someone who definitely had their "one moment in time" as Whitney Houston so eloquently put it are:

Don't follow processes to the extent that you miss the opportunity which is right in front of you.

Yes, he was part of a bidding team and yes, he needed to put more 20ps in the meter but I was in a tiny lift with him for goodness sake and didn't say anything. I now realise what a fantastic opportunity that was to ask him things like "what was it like to score a hat trick in a world cup final?" or "How does being an iconic figure affect your life?" Small things like that. What was I thinking?!

There have been several studies about what happens when individuals come through the door of the office in the morning. During Covid, the doors swung less frequently of course and it will be interesting to see if the passing through the "virtual office doors" by logging on from home has a similar impact.

Some of the studies relate to the behavioural shifts that people exhibit when they move from their domestic environment into their work environment.

One of the things I found interesting was the extent to which people follow rules/processes when at work regardless of the outcome and how that contrasts with what they might do in their private lives. There were some suggestions that people are more likely to follow rules in a work situation even if they think that logically it should be done differently and even if they see that the outcome of following the process could be very bad for someone else.

In other words, people are more likely to blindly follow processes when they are at work and as a result miss the opportunity to improve the outcome.

How crazy is that?

Well, on one level, looked at form one perspective, it's not particularly crazy at all. I mean, if we didn't have processes where would we be? More pertinently, if we had no confidence that people would follow our processes then where would that leave us when it came to communication with shareholders, regulators and other stakeholders?

Processes have been put in place for effectiveness, efficiency or other admirable reasons so it is helpful to have confidence that people will follow them.

Sometimes, you don't want people to think too much, do you?

"Just get the job done... following the standard process, please".

If the process has been designed by someone sensible then it is likely to do exactly what you want it to, most of the time.

I say "most of the time" because here's the rub. What about justifiable exceptions that the process has not been designed to allow?

"The computer says 'no' " ...even though it is bleedin' obvious to everyone that the right answer should be 'yes'.

In many situations, the best thing for everyone would be for the employee to see that the process is producing an unintended outcome and be confidence enough to make an exception in an appropriate way.

In high volume process environments involving humans, it can be difficult to accommodate this. Targets need to be met and it can be easier to allow a "process crash" for a particular individual customer than it can be to give it the full time care and attention it might reasonably need to produce the "right outcome". Yes, the "right outcome" doesn't always equal the "best outcome" and a mature conversation about risk needs to accept levels of possible 'failure'.

There is an increasingly rich field of knowledge out there on how to best deal with these types of challenge, which was ignited by the financial crisis over a decade ago and is now having its flames fanned by the procedural chaos of dealing with Covid 19.

Whatever the art of seeing the bigger picture, the simple lesson is that blindly following procedure is at your own peril because the opportunity for achieving better might go unnoticed.

Is there really a process you need to follow or have you just made one up in your head?

What process was I actually "following" in the first place? There was no process which prohibited me from having a chat with Geoff so why had I apparently made one up in my head and, in my youthful exuberance, convinced myself to follow it so that he didn't have an 'advantage' (which of course he wouldn't have got if I had engaged him in a more fruitful, for me, conversation)?

Notwithstanding the importance of processes which I touched on in the first tip from this encounter, there are times when people imagine a process to be in place which isn't actually there.

A classic is "we can't do that for insurance reasons". That type of statement implies that there is some form of process in place which explicitly states that the activity cannot be undertaken because, if it did, insurance protection would be invalidated and that would be enough to dissuade the company from undertaking the activity.

There will no doubt be some situations where that is exactly the case.

However, in other situations, it will be nothing more than a well-intended guess about the operation of the insurance protection (and the organisation's reliance on it) and one which can get in the way of risks being taken (even if possible resulting adverse events would not be covered by insurance in the first place).

People make up procedures which don't actually exist all the time.

"Health & Safety wouldn't let us do that" is another one frequently used. In some instances, I'm very sure that those safeguarding our health and safety would not want something to happen, but in other instances they might well be prepared to accept that the risks posed to health and safety are reasonable and, assuming they can see evidence that the risks have been properly managed (i.e. identified, assessed, controlled and monitored) would actually be quite prepared to allow the activity to happen.

I wonder just how many opportunities have been lost, not because of Health & Safety specialists saying 'no' but people believing that Health & Safety specialists would have put in place some sort of rule to prevent it from happening, when actually no such procedure or rule was in place or deemed necessary.

Maybe it would not be unreasonable when someone makes a statement about some preventative rule or process being in place, to just "check it out" before a final decision is made?

It might just occasionally throw up the realization that the risks can be taken and there is no procedure to have to follow after all.

Occasionally, uncovering that no procedure exists comes as something other than a pleasant surprise. From time to time, digging deeper to understand the procedures in place can result in the discovery that no procedure actually exists where one definitely should. That could be because an old procedure was no longer relevant or had become obsolete in some other way but it could also be that something had simply "fallen between the cracks" of organizational silos and resulted in a procedural gap which really needs to be plugged.

In my encounter with Geoff Hurst, I was thinking in the right way - sort of. I was aware of the need to remain impartial even in the presence of true legends and could see that there should be some form of procedure in place to cover that situation... even if I was unaware of the detail. Whether there actually was such a process in place or not I can't remember but, for goodness sake, shouldn't it have been obvious (even to me) that some degree of chat... or even warmth... would have been okay?

Some people... honestly - their imagination runs away with them.

Everyone needs some sort of second career

This is a short tip. Whether for their own sanity or for financial reasons, nearly everyone will probably need some sort of second career.

Whether you are a risk taker, someone who helps others take risks, someone who stops others taking certain risks, someone who keeps score on risks being taken or someone how conducts independent assurance on how well risks are being managed, the chances are you won't carry on doing the same sort of thing in the same organization for all of your working lives. Even if you want to, the circumstances around you might make it impossible.

The world is changing too fast for us to confident otherwise.

So regardless of whether your "second career" is with the same organization or with a similar role in a different organization or, as in Geoff's case, a very different type of role in a very different type of company in a very different industry, it's worth having a think every now and again about the sorts of scenarios which could occur.

A bit of personal risk management when it comes to your own career might not go amiss. It will probably highlight the importance of your network and put the importance of existing business acquaintances into proper context.

It might help you take the right risks at the right time in your career or help you take what might otherwise be complete leaps of faith into unknown career territory.

Geoff made the transition between careers successfully but many of his fellow footballers from that era did not. Maybe he was lucky but maybe he managed the risks of transition well and better than many.

I'm sure Geoff helped others make career transitions drawing on his own personal experience but I'm pretty sure he is not going to be there for me or you.

I urge you to think about it though as sooner or later a change will come around and those who manage the risks of career transition best are likely to be the winners on a financial and psychological level.

LinkedIn article:

The opportunity to innovate is perhaps greater than it has ever been in my lifetime. The digital shifts happening now provide a platform for anyone who can understand at least some of the potential and seize the opportunity to do something special.

Bringing things together like never before can spark great creativity which can lead to excitement and delight in others and I for one am up for that. I love it.

However, when it comes to innovation in relation to strategy mapping, people & behaviour and risk management, I think I might have misunderstood something which is really important for making it happen... until now, that is.

This sudden realisation has been empowering and that's why I want to share my thoughts with you. To understand my point, you will need to think laterally, in a non-binary fashion and with an open mind so if that's not your thing then don't read any further.

Ready? Okay, here's the issue.

You see, I used to think that a nice Venn diagram would usefully describe the areas of opportunity for progress relating to Strategy Mapping, People & Behaviour and Risk Management.

...but I don't think it does. Let me show you what I mean.

This is what I used to think described the opportunity –
the overlaps in the Venn diagram below.

I used to think these areas of overlap were where the
innovation opportunity and action was for these three sets
of corporate activity.

I don't quite think that way anymore… at least not for
many (and possibly most) organizations. The reason I've
changed my mind on it is that I don't think there actually
are overlaps of this nature in practice in those
organisations. For many organisations, a more accurate
depiction of activity is the following (which I understand
to be more Euler than Venn):

Silos exist in many cases and there is no overlap of activity. Whoops! As a result, the opportunity to innovate can't be described as being inside any of the circles (or "spheres") of confidence and/or competence of practitioners. The situation is similar in increasingly large consulting firms where one diseconomy of scale can be the emergence of such silos (and maybe that is one of the many reasons why we rarely see true thought leadership from those firms in this space anymore).

That's not a good recipe for innovation, is it?

Silos exist in many cases and there is no overlap...

Yes, many will argue there SHOULD be overlaps as, for example, risk management SHOULD be embedded in strategy related work etc (indeed others will argue that, at least informally, there are always overlaps as people have always managed risk one way or another, forever) but it seems to me that reality doesn't always cope well with what "should" be and these old arguments don't need to constrain our pursuit of innovation... even if they are valid.

Wait a minute, though… we are seeing some innovation happening and I've been involved with it with some clients so what is occurring in those organizations and is there a way to depict that diagrammatically?

I think there is and it is still via a Venn (by the way, I know the outline rectangles are missing from all my diagrams but they are not important to the point I'm making). Here is what I deem to be a better visual representation of what needs to happen for smart innovation in this space:

You see, it's not about overlaps in terms of what people currently do (as represented by circles in the earlier Venn. Euler). Okay, in some rare cases it might result in some innovation but stay with me on this.

Instead of overlaps from existing activity, it seems to me

that we need to do new things – beyond current activity – in order to spark the collaboration, creativity and energy for innovation. We need to create overlaps and that means people doing new things so that real world gaps (Euler) can be bridged and possible overlaps created (Venn). The expansion of circles into petals in the above Venn is intended to represent doing new things to create overlaps.

...we need to do new things... in order to spark the collaboration, creativity and energy for innovation

---

Now, I know some of you will think that this is all semantics and that bringing together Strategy Mapping, People & Behaviour and Risk Management is not that difficult because overlaps already exist and that playing around with the shape of the Venn circles doesn't really make any difference. Maybe those of you thinking that are right because maybe there are at least some overlaps in some firms. Then again, maybe you are not because I believe that this way of thinking helps shine light on the way forward… even for firms where some overlaps already exist but where new overlaps could be productive.

The key point in all of this is that for many organizations, looking for the overlaps for those involved in Strategy Mapping, People & Behaviour and Risk Management to innovate is likely to lead to disappointment… because there are few. Asking each of them to do more than they currently do though (ie some new things) in order that overlaps can then exist and consequent opportunities exploited might just be a better way.

> *...reality doesn't always cope well
> with what "should" be*

Now I've shown you the point visually, through the diagrams above, I hope you find the mindset helpful in discovering routes to innovation.

Do you agree with me?

You might be asking "what are those new things and, really importantly, how can you actually persuade people to do them? You can find out for yourself or get in touch if you'd welcome my input.

Ciao!

Sometimes it is a little bit scary to stand alone on a bridge... especially if those on either side of the chasm just stay at their end and stare at you.   It can feel vulnerable to leave the safety of the cliff edge and step out onto a bridge - especially one which has only just been built to a new and unproven design.

Standing in the middle of the bridge looking at both sides and wondering if any of them will show your courage and also come onto the bridge, takes a bit of doing.

To set up camp on the bridge to show your commitment to the meeting of both sides can also be risky, not least because you are no longer seen as a member of either tribe.

In many organisations, bridging is for the brave. Coming out of one silo and trying to build a bridge with another can be difficult.   Suggesting new connections and synergies can be tricky if the majority would prefer to stay in their silo (which they frequently do).

For many years I had looked at the relationship between risk management in strategy. I remember being shocked about the absence of quality risk information in strategy documents from top strategy consulting firms. I could also see that many risk functions were being unsuccessful in securing a position in relation to strategy setting and mapping. A bridge was necessary there.

Then there was the people element. Like the other two elements in the Venn diagram, it was getting attention but the link with strategy (especially when it comes to the behaviour of people) was often weak and as for people risk (ie the relationship between people and risk management) well, it was also - how can I say it nicely - underdeveloped.

It's frustrating when logically obvious linkages are not made.

I wrote this article to try and draw attention to this lack of logic in common practice.

It was easy enough to come up with the "Whoops" diagram which I thought captured the point about the disconnects really well, even if I do say so myself. It was while struggling to move the shapes around to come up with a more integrated diagram on Powerpoint that helped crystalize my thought that it wasn't overlapping of existing activity which was needed. Rather, it was new activity which was needed to build the bridges. The new activity could be the thing which sparked the improved collaboration towards successful achievement of strategy.

Doing new stuff that nobody has done before in your department or organisation though, is essentially walking out onto the bridge... it takes courage as well as imagination and creativity.

Look at what big data is doing to our world though. Creating linkages from previously unlinked activity is sparking some very valuable initiatives. Some of the richest people in the world got their wealth partly from joining up systems and data which were previously not joined up.

When I wrote the article, I could see that there was so much opportunity to be exploited from new connections but if everyone stayed on their side of the bridge(s) then the spark wouldn't happen.

So what was needed then and still needed now? Well, let me suggest a few things which even today are still not particularly commonplace in organisations but which I think would make a difference on the three dimensions in the diagram.

- Set and revise strategy with insightful consideration of risks in and of the strategy
- Create strategy maps and implementation plans which directly link risk management activity to the drivers of strategic success ie deal with the risks to strategy
- Formally consider if and how well-established behavioural change techniques could be used at different stages in the implementation of strategy and build them into your strategy maps
- Articulate how people risk undermines all other risk management activity in your organization
- Craft an approach to people risk management which can be embedded in the broader approach to risk management in the organization and linked directly to drivers of strategic success

For your see, be amazed my friends, these logically obvious things are typically not done that well, if at all in many organisations.

What about the risk management lessons from this article? Well, I think they are probably as follows:

- Paradoxically, activity relating to strategy, people and risk management doesn't overlap that well in many organisations
- In order to spark opportunity, new activity is needed in strategy, people and risk management activity to provide overlaps as the groundwork
- All hail the "bridgers". Those are the brave people who really make the difference.

11

LinkedIn article:

There is a fantastic array of tools and techniques available nowadays to shed more light on the complexities of human behaviour, isn't there?

Ranging from neuroscience on why people see peril faster than joy; to psychometric profiling which provides indications of risk-taking type and the extent to which people are likely to follow rules; and to data analytics on relationship quality between individuals and departments; it seems more insight is becoming available on human behaviour in organizations and the extent to which it is influenced by those organizations.

Maybe we have the ability to understand people risk better than we did before.

Some supervisors are now talking about the usefulness of behavioural change techniques in influencing culture. Some major transformation programs now include formal consideration of how these techniques can be used at different stages in the program. Specialists in the use of such techniques are now connecting better with those running the business.

Maybe we are on our way to a state-of-the-art uplift across financial services on this.

What then of the assessment and control of people risk – and that portion of the operational risk capital charge (people) which arguably poses greater uncertainty than the others (processes, systems, external events)?

This should perhaps be encapsulated in the operational risk and control self-assessment (ORCSA) and related frameworks which have been developed by firms since... well, maybe not actually that long ago for financial services firms – what, the mid 90's?

Should we therefore expect that the improved understanding of people risk (and what can be used to influence it) will be reflected in those ORCSA? In the risk lists, risk assessments, control descriptions, improvement actions?

Of course, there is probably an economic limit on how much should be spent in advancing understanding of people risk. Data is becoming cheaper though and if some tools claim to provide say a 30% reliable indicator of risk related behaviour then should effective use of such tools result in a reduction to the operational risk capital charge (and/or other capital charges if people risk is also included in distributions for those)?

Might this be People Risk 2.0? I think it could be and in the long run I feel it is quite likely – but timing is always more difficult to predict... partly because of what it means to be human, operating in chaotic systems with other humans!

People risks have been included in risk and control assessments since they were first used.

At one level, people get it. They understand that there are risks associated with your people. They can see that people need to be appropriately trained and suitably qualified and they also understand that people might do unexpected things (intentionally or unintentionally).

Those familiar with financial services will recognize people risk as a subcomponent of operational risk and understand that overall levels of riskiness should influence the size of the capital safety nets which those types of organisations are required to hold - just in case. The article was written with those businesses in mind as you can probably tell by the references to the capital charges and the teasing possibility of the capital requirements being reduced if new information shines new light on the level of people risk.

Although the article was written for financial services, the non-capital charge bits of it are equally as relevant to non-FS organisations and if you are form one of those then you will probably recognize people risk as a category from some of the risk assessment work you have done because can there be anyone of working age in the land who has not participated in a risk assessment of one form or another (even if the design or execution of it was poor)?

Here is the thing, organisations tend to think of people risk as a standalone risk category and treat it as such on their risk assessments. It isn't though.

I mean you can address it that way but that misses something really important, which is that people risk impacts all other risks in one way, shape or form.

Think about it - the identification, assessment and economic control of all risks is undermined by uncertainty associated with people (people risk) and conversely underpinned by the quality of people risk management undertaken.

So how might that relationship be better reflected in risk assessments?

Well in simple terms, rather than being a separate risk or risk category, the uncertainties associated with people could be included as part of the assessment of each of the other risks and risk categories. Similarly, when controls are being attached to those other risks, variability of human behaviour could be taken into account and specifically documented. When evaluation of risks and control takes place then data inputs relating to the human element could be taken into account - thus enabling the relationship between people risk and all other risks to be reflected in the broader assessments.

There can be more sophisticated ways of assessing risks and controls of course but the principle of addressing people risk in the above way can stand in those too.

Since I wrote the article, there has been some inflation on People Risk version numbers with 2.0 becoming 3.0 for another writer and I think even 4.0 for yet another.

Personally, I'd just like to see 2.0 happen in most organization because it's not that difficult to do - it just requires a little bit of effort thinking it through and making it happen. The result would be more insightful risk assessments and improved understanding of how people risk impacts other risks. That would lead to greater understanding of how money spent on improving people risk flows through into confidence of meeting strategic objectives.

I think the people risk 2.0 tips could therefore be as follows:
- People risk undermines all other risks
- Make sure your risk and control assessments consider people risk as part of the assessment of other risks and not as a separate risk category.

12

LinkedIn article:

Changing world. Changing strategy. Changing risk. Changing risk management?

Maybe we have all four. Certainly, the first three get lots of attention. What about the fourth? It gets some attention too, doesn't it? As change is all around us, and people are increasingly "up for" those changes, could now be the best time in a generation to achieve more breakthroughs in risk management?

There are lots of ideas around for step changes in improving risk management. For example:

1. The inclusion of more behavioural knowledge, data and capability in operational risk and control self-assessments
2. Structured consideration and use of behavioural change techniques for influencing culture
3. Creative use of data including semantic data
4. Just-in-time, mobile enabled video learning for policy awareness and other risk-related needs
5. Alternatives to the three lines of defence model which would work better and make responsibilities clearer
6. More robust risk management effectiveness measures that take into account the risk management processes, the people operating them and the way in which they are tailored for underlying business processes in an integrated, not separate, way
7. Sharper linking of risk management

prioritization to agility in business strategy

Is adoption of these types of improvements keeping pace with the changes in strategy and risk we are all witnessing? We know that people often want change but aren't prepared to change. It is sometimes difficult to think differently about risk management and/or difficult to change things in practice when monthly or quarterly cycles create pressure to maintain the status quo. It can be difficult to achieve a shift, even where the logic for improvement is strong.

Tying risk management prioritization back to strategy has made good progress since the early 2000s when the risk section of strategy papers often consisted of nothing more than a couple of bullet points. Those strategies are changing big time though, aren't they? Not all of them, granted, but many of them. The world is changing a lot. Strategies are changing a lot. Maybe people are open to more radical changes in strategy than previously. Maybe people are therefore more open to radical changes in risk management approaches than previously.

If that's true then maybe it should be easier to make significant advances in risk management now, when so much else is changing, than it has been since the dotcom boom ended.

Bring it on... are you up for it?

You'll recognize some of the items in this numbered-list type post from some of my other posts... nothing wrong with a bit of repetition now and again to make sure people are paying attention, is there?

103

As I say, there is nothing wrong with a bit of repetition now and again so hold back on pointing that out and trying to claim some of your money back on this book!

The key thing I wanted to draw out from this article relates to the change occurring in the world. I make the point that with so much change happening all around us, surely there will be more acceptance of the need for change in risk management.

Some will no doubt argue that risk management needs to remain stable when everything around them is changing so much and to that I'd simply respond;

'Don't be stupid'

...and I'd mean it too.

I'd like to think that people are more open to risk management change when everything else is changing because the logic is strong and if the organization already ties it's risk management activity directly to drivers of strategy then they will automatically be highlighted as needing review as the strategic drivers will be changing anyway.

Then again, if the organisation does not already tie its activity directly to drivers of strategy then the review might not be so automatic and I'd take a wild guess, based on my experience, that there will actually be a lot of organisations in that boat.

Come on though, whether you are a risk specialist or not, we can all take the opportunity during periods of fundamental change to review, enhance and improve what we do to manage risk.

No, that sounds too reactive an approach... how about this instead?

Everything is changing, Batman, let's get out there and get our stuff done as part of the big switch!

...is that better?

How would you put it?

Rather than just listing some tips based on the seven items in the post, I think the main tips could be as follows:

- Look at how your organisation's strategy and strategy drivers are all changing as a result of the fourth industrial revolution
- Tie your risk management improvement activity to those changing factors and you shouldn't go far wrong

13

LOUIS ARMSTRONG & TONY BENNET - "...I see friends shake hands, saying 'how do you do?'...they're really saying 'I love you...'"

I was in a professional stage show once which toured the U.S.A.

Our 56 performances stretched across 10 weeks and we did shows in 28 states. When I tell you the entire first two weeks were spent in California and the last week in Florida, you'll get a rough idea of the miles we cracked up in the 7 weeks sandwiched in between!

I can't say for certain but I'm pretty sure that I remember the coach driver saying that our bus was new when he picked us up but would essentially be written off by the end of the tour because the mileage was so high.

Yes, dear friends, how we travelled and in such style... cramped on a bus every day with all our personal luggage plus the show's costumes, equipment and props etc either in the luggage hold or at the back of the bus itself.

Ah yes, the easy life of showbiz. Apart from those easy weeks at the beginning and the end of the tour a typical day went something like this:

08:00 - Breakfast
08.30 - Pack your stuff on the bus and let's go
17:00 - Arrive at the next motel/hotel and unpack your stuff
17:30 - Get on the bus and travel to the venue
17:45 - Arrive at the venue and unpack and set up the entire show
19:00 - Do the show
22:00 - Pack the show back onto the bus
22:30 - Look for something to eat

24:00 - Go to bed (or stay up drinking)

You get the idea. Essentially, this was on repeat for, well, months.

Sometimes, we arrived late and had to go straight to the venue rather than stopping at the motel.

It's not that I was complaining at the time (or since). Certainly not.

Can you imagine being paid to see some of the most fantastic, beautiful and diverse scenery on the planet even if it was mostly from the inside of a bus jam-packed with the same 26 people you had been with 24 hours per day for those months?

To top it all, we got to perform in some absolutely fantastic theatres with some amazing history and in a couple of occasions, big stadia. Those venues certainly made up for the rough ones we also visited although the show was always basically the same regardless of the surroundings.

There were touches of the "Forest Gump" about things too. When we were all so tired to bother about where we were going next we'd take the opportunity sleep on the bus and would wake up to discover which "chocolate we were getting from the box". Would it be a big fancy one with all the lighting and sound equipment you can imagine or a nasty one where the black tab curtains has been slashed by some disillusioned youth?

We didn't know, or need to know, what was coming next... which in retrospect was also an absolute luxury!

Talking of luxury, I remember we were performing at the Hershey Theatre in Hershey, Pennsylvania... chocolate town! It's a lovely, ornate theatre with a hint of gothic around the stage. It's also quite big but that is beside the point.

In the "green room" backstage and downstairs, our hosts were good enough to provide some refreshments and yep, you guessed it - slap bang in the middle of the table was a big, big, big bowl of Hershey chocolate including more Peppermint Patties than I've ever seen in one big pile! Our lead singers couldn't eat the chocolate during the performance but we got stuck in and I think the sugar helped us make the decision as to whether to take the stairs or the old elevator up to stage level. Stairs or elevator? I mean, what could possibly go wrong if you were using an old-fashioned lift to get to the state in time for your cue? We took the stairs.

People often as what was my favourite city.

After many years travelling there for work purposes, I realized that my favourite city is New York, New York. Oh yes brothers and sisters... The Big Apple... the city that never sleeps. I find it one of the most exciting, stimulating and energizing cities on the planet.

That's now.

Back in the day though, after the tour which was I think 1991, I didn't point to any city when people asked me the question. Instead, I always said that what I enjoyed most was not the big cities but "the real America" and by that I meant some of the smallest towns we visited and performed in. The sorts of towns tourists don't normally see because they don't normally go there.

I loved them because of the warm feeling that (most of them) gave me. I don't think it was the white chapels or the tree lined residential streets that did it and it certainly wasn't the ubiquitous K-marts (although they did come in very handy on several occasions like when suitcases gave way or we felt the need to buy a baseball and glove).

It was none of those things.

It was the people that I loved and it is funny how some things stick with you such that you remember them years on.

One night we had performed in a small theatre somewhere. I can't remember where the gig was or what the theatre was like but what I do remember was that the "Chairman of the theatre's organizing committee" had booked for the entire cast to go to the local bar afterwards to receive some pre-ordered pizza. That, my friends was like Christmas day (if you are that way inclined).

Rather than being abandoned to find the nearest McDonalds or slightly upmarket eatery, here we were being hosted like never before and there was I sitting next to and having a chat with the Chairman himself who happened to also be the local undertaker. Note "the" rather than "a" local undertaker for there was only one.

What a lovely chap he was too. Genuinely pleasant and one of humanity's gems.

He was just as appreciative of what we had delivered to the receptive audience in the theatre that night as we were of what he had had delivered to the pub for the receptive cast members to devour.

He told me of some of the entertainers they had hosted over the years and although I recall that the list was pretty good for such a small place, I only member one of the people on it.

The Chairman was not one to "blow his own trumpet" as the expression goes but that night, in the cosy bar he told me of someone who definitely did. Perhaps the most famous trumpet player of all time, Louis Armstrong. Ol' Satchmo!

Now what you don't know is that the LP I played most and essentially wore out the vinyl on when I was studying for my degree in risk management was a Louis Armstrong album! Louis had sadly died many years previously but to be in a direct conversation with someone who had done the same with Louis Armstrong was awesome.

I have never and will never forget the kindness of those people in that lovely place and my once-removed encounter with someone who, for many reasons, was one of the greatest musical entertainers the world has seen.

Talking of which, have you heard of Tony Bennet? Of course you have. A fabulous A-list old crooner. "Chicago, Chicago" or "I left my heart... in San Francisco"... there are loads of them.

Well, after a few weeks on the road, a pattern started to emerge. Whenever we played a big venue, Tony Bennet was usually due to play the following week. Mysteriously, whenever we played a small venue, Tony was not due to be playing in the future... I can't think why.

I have to admit, it was quite a thrill to know that Tony Bennet was going to be on after us. I mean, it's one thing playing at a theatre where many of the greats have performed in the past. It really is brilliant to do that but it is something else altogether when you know that the legend is on next!

The trouble was, he was always on the week after us so we never met him. One of the cast did leave a special letter for him - tucked behind one of those dressing room mirrors which has all the bulbs around it - but whether he got the message or not we shall never know.

Yes, despite being "chased around the USA" by Tony Bennet we were never able to let him catch us.

They say timing is everything and that's one of my tips from my tour.

Timing is everything

On the one hand, had we been able to change the dates a bit we might have met Tony Bennet. On the other hand, had we changed the dates, we wouldn't have been able to perform in the first place because he was on. We certainly got a thrill from knowing he was next on and we wouldn't have got that if he was due 'in six months' so, there were probably some good and bad bits to our timing.

Timing is important from a risk management perspective. Sometimes it's because if you don't place your bets early enough then the great big croupier in the sky won't let you play in the game. You've got to be in it to win it and if you miss your chance it can be gone forever. That means there isn't always time to fully understand the odds.

Timing is also important in other ways. Sometimes there is "no point in closing the stable door after the horse as bolted". We all know about the "benefit of hindsight" and "no use crying over spilt milk". There are plenty of well-known sayings which have temporal risk management undertones to them.

In politics, we've all witnessed a spokesman following up a bad incident with the words "what's happened is in the past, what we must now do is ensure this never happens again" which some might say is another phrase for "blimey, we should have anticipated this and done something about it before it was too late but we can't admit to that so let's make promises we can't or won't keep about risk management in the future".

In a corporate sense, "too late" is an unwelcome visitor from a risk management perspective.

Let's start at the top - shouldn't strategy be set with due regard to risk? You'd think so, wouldn't you? At one level, it typically is of course but it's amazing how light the consideration of risk can actually be when strategy is set. Risk management specialists are often not included early enough in the process to make a difference - even if they were capable of doing so in the first place which is not always a given.

Leaving the technical aspects of the two-way interplay between risk and strategy aside for now, it probably should be happening at the time that strategy is set and then a different aspect of risk management considered when strategy maps and consequent implementation plans are being drafted.

Similar considerations should also apply during the annual planning process or in major project setup... but it is currently common practice for risk only to be appreciated (and even then maybe not fully) a bit further down the road.

Considering risks as an afterthought is criminally negligent in some instances which is why there is of course some time given to certain aspects of risk (particularly those relating to health & safety etc but only in some countries) but it beats me why there isn't better consideration of broader strategic risks (or risks to strategy) right up-front.

If you are a risk specialist and trying to break in to the strategy setting process (and the other activities mentioned above) then you will know how important timing of your involvement is and you might also be aware that "teaching old dogs new tricks" isn't always the easiest sell in the world. That's why having a good grasp of psychology and behavioural change techniques can come in useful but that, as they say, is another can of worms.

Even at a basic level, choosing your moment to raise a challenge relating to risk is important. Ideally, you want to allow enough time for the person you've challenged to take onboard your challenge and deal with the solution options you are suggesting (you have provided some options for a solution too haven't you?).

Raising the issue too late isn't always helpful.   You know the sort of thing... you're all in a meeting and seem to be making good progress when three minutes before the end someone chucks in a thought, idea, worry or challenge leaving no time for it to be resolved and everyone is left wondering what they should do with it. Some people enjoy lobbing in these verbal "hand-grenades" and others just feel the need to throw it in before the end of the meeting. Really skilled operators don't do that because it leaves things too unsettled with no time to refocus and prioritise.

In other words, and in pretty basis terms, the tip is don't just hurl in risk considerations at the end... get them properly positioned and/or signposted early when there is still time to take action to ensure the risk being taken is understood.

You might be right about everything in risk management but if your timing is out then you might not get the perfect result you seek.

Legends live on

I was a baby when Louis Armstrong died and yet there I was as a fully-grown adult being thrilled by my "once-removed conversation" via the undertaker. Louis' own career spanned five decades but the impact of what he did has lasted much longer. I wonder if he felt he left jazz in a better place than he found it and I wonder who could feel the same about the art and science of risk management.

Beyond those macro musings about risk management influence, there is a lot to be found in more micro environments. In the early 90s there were some "legends" of risk management in what, compared to now, was a very small risk management industry. They had heated debates at conferences, contributed articles for trade journals and took the trouble to write letters to the editor on some pretty important issues where the emergence of a more formalised approach to risk management was making a difference. One such example of a topic was should the Chief Risk Officer be accountable for risk management in an organisation? More than 30 years later, the jury is still out on that one in some organisations... and even those who are clear that the CEO and not the CRO has responsibility, sometimes struggle to deal with more granular details on accountabilities across management teams for dealing with risk - because risk is inherent in everyone's activities.

Most of those who greatly influenced the early years of formalised risk management in the UK (and I think globally because in terms of overall Enterprise Risk Management, it seemed that the UK was streaks ahead of any other country at that time... at least in terms of thought leadership and know-how) took their curtain calls on the risk management stage a while ago but the thing is - they did move it all forward and set risk management on its sure but bumpy course.

Legendary risk takers have been around for ages of course, but legendary risk management (as we know it today) thought leaders are a more recent phenomenon.

It's hard to become a risk management thought leader. What is thought leadership anyway? Are survey results thought leadership or just the results of a survey? Is research thought leadership or just a verification of history? Are ideas thought leadership even if they are rubbish?

Hmm... and is the market ready for your thought leadership? Does acceptance of risk management improvement opportunity imply admission of current risk management being sub-standard and if it does, does that scare off would-be consumers of your thought leadership?

There was a time when the "Big 4" accounting-based consulting firms produced a good output of risk management thought leadership but now they are so much larger, they need to feed themselves with projects which are typically much bigger than risk management thought leadership usually produces. Nowadays, it looks like most risk management thought leadership comes from independent consultants whose business model is far more suited to resulting client projects.

My own view is that more ideas and creativity based thought leadership would help move things along again... resulting in better risk management in many places but we need the right environments to support that type of activity and at the end of the day, that comes down to hard cash so whatever the ideas and creations, they need to be deemed of value even if the immediate value of risk management improvements can be difficult to demonstrate (because they relate to an uncertain future).

Arise risk management thought leaders of tomorrow, but only if you can find someone to pay for it!

To everyone else, I'd say cherish true risk management thought leaders even if you don't agree with them. Like some of those risk management thought leaders from the late 80s and early 90s, we will miss them when they are gone.

People are people

It's easy to worry about things when it comes to risk management... that's often what you are paid to do, whether or not you are a risk management specialist.

When it comes to people, it's easy to worry about them too. After all, it's their behaviour which drives the bits of risk that you can control. What they do, what they fail to do, how they make judgements, how they prioritise activity, how they operate... it can all be variable and therefore something to address if you want to be confident in your degree of confidence (and that's not as much of a paradox as you might think at first glance!)

There are some league tables around ranking professions in terms of the trust that others have in them. Nursing usually rates pretty highly with politicians, and certain types of journalists at the other end. Trends develop over time and bankers have certainly sunk a bit over the past couple of decades. They are all sweeping generalisations of course (and when it comes to risk management we should all beware sweeping generalisations!). Following the financial crisis around 2008, the culture in banks and the behavioural traits which accompanied them came under much scrutiny. Just about everyone was sure we needed to do something about it but very few people made suggestions as to how to bring *it* about.

I think there probably were some bad bankers around although the degree of evilness they exhibited seems to depend heavily on your personal point of view - your ethics and own professional standards etc.

Let's not go into the regulatory/legal recriminations... or what some might point to as the lack of.

Fraud risk is an area which nearly always appears in risk management framework material - both internal and external frauds. Combined with money laundering it presents significant toxicity on our planet.

So there is plenty to worry about from a risk management perspective when it comes to people because humans can be unpredictable and some do bad things.

However, it's worth keeping mind that most people are full of good intent.

I remember being in Ecuador as part of the British Week celebrations there in the early 90s. A member of staff form the British Council there asked me at the end of the week what I thought about the people I had met there.

Keep in mind that you can sometimes feel like a celebrity yourself when you visit areas of poverty and people try to attract your attention and money from the minute you arrive. I can see why some people would get carried away with that but it was a stark reminder to me that whatever grumblings I had about my own upbringing and no matter how much criticism I could levy at my own home town's shortcomings, I was forever lucky to have been born away from true poverty.

Years later, I was reminded of just how lucky I am when travelling through poorer parts of Mumbai. It's not a movie, those people on the other side of the taxi's window are desperate.

Anyway, back to my youthful foray to Ecuador where I had gone with my dear old Dad who had been there on previous years to play his bagpipes during the event. You know he was such a lovely man and at his funeral a couple of decades later (where despite it being such short notice, several hundred people turned up to show their respects) the recurring messages of support talks about how much of a lovely gentleman he was.

I was trying to be cool of course because I was pumping full of hormones so in retrospect, I don't think I was all that great a companion to my dad on that trip although my mum said he never mentioned it and had actually

117

enjoyed the experience with me. It's funny how things stick in your brains sometimes and although I'm glad I went and had that adventure with him, I still feel a little bit guilty about what I now see as my immature behaviour at the time... and it was all well before "Jack Whitehall's Travels with My Father" made it easier to celebrate individual differences while on tour!

The guy from the British Council asked me the question in the back of a taxi going back to the hotel after an event at a school. I kid you not, the windscreen had a bullet hole in it and the back door was only held close by a tiny bolt lock of the type that your grandparents probably had in their toilet in the 50s.

I thought about his question.

"What do I think about the people? I think people are people... although the circumstances are specific, underneath it all we are all humans and we are the same."

He turned to the front and looked out at the above-ground graves on the hillsides and said "That's a good way to look at it, Clive - that's absolutely right".

So people are people and most people are good and if you remember that then it can help in all sorts of ways. You might trust people more at work. You might find it easier to make business contacts etc.

They might be trying to build links with you too (and one of the things that Covid-19 has reminded us of is the importance of networks) so maybe be ready to trust them as your default. Yes, keep an eye out for the baddies but believe they have good intentions as your default setting.

They say dogs never forget acts of kindness and I think it might be the same for humans (even if they don't fully appreciate it at the time). It is the people who go the extra mile to make you feel welcome, valued and appreciated that secure the positive place in your story and your very being... like that undertaker somewhere in the USA.

14

THERE WERE FIVE GUYS IN THE RAT PACK – AND THERE ARE FIVE RISK LASERS TO SHINE ON MAJOR CHANGE PROGRAMS

> **LinkedIn article:**
>
> Hi everybody! If you are like most people, you won't be able to name all five guys or all five lasers, first time around. That's okay. Just remember that there are five though so that you don't get caught out in any sort of question session where you'd want to be confident with your answer.
>
> Did you get all five? If you did - well done. That's right... 1) Frank Sinatra, 2) Sammy Davis Jr, 3) Dean Martin... no wait, that's not what you were interested in, right? You were more interested in the five risk lasers for major change projects.
>
> Okay, here we go; 1) Risks to the successful delivery of the project - usually in some form of risk register 2) Risk deltas as a result of the project... less frequently documented. Got it so far? Good... and what are the other three?
>
> I claimed (and it was a bold claim) that there were five main risk lasers to shine on major change programs (you know, programs like cost reduction initiatives, post-merger integrations, digital transformations) and I claimed that there were five guys in the Rat Pack. You might choose to disagree on both – that's okay – I agree it is debatable although the discussion on the Rat Pack is probably more settled than the risk lasers one.
>
> So, back to the list of risk lasers... 3) Detachment and

reattachment of operational controls during and after transition… people often forget to plan and execute on that one 4) Risk management framework components in the business (eg risk appetite monitoring) being impacted by the proposed changes?

For the Rat Pack, people often forget about Peter Lawford. Many people over a certain age have never heard of Joey Bishop and yet he was the fifth member of the Rat Pack (that's "The Clan" version for Rat Pack aficionados). He was also the one who outlived the others by the way… with his cat, Misty. He was also funny.

> *"Many programs operate without consideration of all five which... seems illogical"*

Okay so if Joey Bishop was the fifth member of the Rat Pack, what is the fifth risk laser? 5) Changes to the Risk Management Function (Department) as a result of the proposed major change program (e.g. as a result of headcount/cost reduction).

There we go, five risk lasers to think about shining when planning for a major change program. If they had to be sequenced to fit with the typical steps of a major change program, I think it could be sensible to consider them in the following order: 5-2-4-1-3 and the relationships are probably more "start to start" than "end to start".

Many programs operate without consideration of all five which, when you think about it as I'm sure you will, seems illogical - except where it's not been done that way in the past which is I suppose some form of perverted logic as to why things are the way they are. The world is changing though so now is the time to make progress.

Five risk lasers... and five guys in the Rat Pack (and "Take That" and "One Direction" come to think of it – Robbie Williams, Gary Barlow, Mark... er... Harry Styles, Liam er... yes, er...).

Share with me what you think.

I should probably declare something early on in respect of this article. The only reason I knew about Joey Bishop was because I was him... for a week.

Let me explain. I had heard of The Rat Pack although I cannot remember if it was before or after I got to know The Brat Pack... the gorgeous group of up-and-coming actors in the 80s.

I was well aware of Frank Sinatra, of course and also Dean Martin and Sammy Davis Jr. I remember them being on the records my grandparents played on their gramophone when I was really young and I also remember the end of some corporate parties in the early 90s when Ol' Blue Eyes' (Sinatra) rendition of "New York, New York" marked the moment to link arms in a big circle and get ready for the collective leg kick (not to be confused with the collective arse-kick that we all got from Covid 19, if you will excuse my foul mouth).

I hadn't heard of the other two until the last show I was in before parking my beloved theatrical hobby for the best part of two decades.

It was, I think, the coolest show I was ever in because it came slap bang in the middle of a resurgence in popularity of the "swing" style of easy listening music and here is how it came about.

122

A fellow hobbyist (who also went on to become a Partner in a large professional services firm) decided to write his own show telling the story of The Rat Pack. It told the tale of all five members although as you'd expect it centred on Frank. Each of the five introduced himself at the beginning of the show before it lurched into a mix of dramatical representations of their private lives coupled with many of the very big musical numbers they were famous for.

I was given the part of Joey Bishop which meant that when the show opened and there was a bright spotlight on each of us, the audience were pretending to listen to the intros from Frank, Dean and Sammy while actually trying to work out who me and the other guy were!

I kind of knew that was coming... not just because I didn't know the other two myself before the show but because when we were handing out flyers in Epsom one Saturday morning, a couple of people came up to me holding the flyer only to ask 'I know the big three and Peter Lawford but who is the other guy?'. When I told them it was Joey, the just looked blank, shrugged and walked off.

It was clear then that people wouldn't know who I was playing in the show until I was introduced although despite my opening line that 'there were five, yes, five guys in The Rat Pack', it wasn't hard to feel the audiences' collective shrug after I told them. They had, after all, paid their money for tickets to hear the famous songs by the famous members of The Rat Pack.

By the way, Joey knew his place although there is a YouTube video of him joking that he was so chuffed to be playing The Sands hotel in Las Vegas with Frank that he agreed to have Frank's name above his on the neon billboard! Many people say he was the comedy genius behind the funny bits which played a big part in the warm and familiar performances by the others.

Anyway, history has already made up its mind about Joey.

The upcoming show was also special because we were due to have a live "big band" playing the numbers for us on stage as we sang and danced.

Unfortunately, the week before the show was due to go on, the band withdrew. Can you imagine? We had sold tickets partly on the promise of a big band so what were we going to do?

The contingency plan up to that point had been drafting in the rehearsal pianist to bang out some chords but everyone knew that 'My Way', 'Come fly with me', 'Ain't that a kick in the head' and all the others would simply be nowhere near as good if instead of a 15 piece big band, we had plinky plonks from the piano. By the way, I love the piano but everything has its place.

Needless to say there were a lot of murmurings, tut-tuts and whatnots as well as general panic.

However, all was not lost because a few days before the show, the dad of one of the cast managed to pursued his own band to play for us instead. That was nothing short of a miracle. Not only did these heroes agree to give up a whole week of evenings to be in the show, they got paid a lot less than they normally would have done... these guys were professionals and actually much better than the original band we had booked.

They were truly fantastic and collectively we blew the audience away every night. Despite the lack of rehearsal time with them, the only dodgy moment in the whole of show week was when I was doing my solo of "Have you met Miss Jones?" all dressed in black tuxedo and backed by some very glamorously dressed lady dancers. It was on Wednesday or Thursday night and for some inexplicable reason the band went off at a speed 50% faster than they were due to.

Had I only been singing, I could have got by easily but - you guessed it - I had to join the ladies in the dance routine as well. Some of the straight-forward bits were easy enough but the spins, oh man, the spins!

Anyway, enough of that. Let's just say that every performance of this show ended with goosebumps and tears as Frank sang 'My Way" with the screaming brass in the band.

Brilliant.

Fifteen or so years later when I was writing the article, it was coincidental that I was trying to introduce readers to five things of which they'd probably only guess a few and it seemed like the opportunity to try and catch eyes with the Rat Pack reference was too good to miss.

In an attempt to bridge between risk management and program management, I'd cleared my mind of the way risk was typically managed in change programs and set about trying to work out how it could be done. What could a risk specialist (internal or otherwise) bring to the management of programs which would improve the way risk was taken?

I came up with the five 'lasers' (or 'lenses' as I called them initially) after a lot of conceptual scribbling and re-scribbling big sheets of blank A3 paper.

That's when I realized the, slightly worrying, truth that many (and I'd guess most) large change programs don't properly address all five aspects of risk.

We all know that many large programs fail to deliver on time and to budget. If we are honest, we probably all also know that those responsible for delivering the programs are not particularly interested in understanding some aspects of risk - they want to know (and convince others) that everything is fine with green dashboards being the typical representation of how everything is up to the moment when it is no longer possible to keep up the illusion and with the flick of a switch (or a click of a mouse, or a tap of a tablet... anyway you get the idea) the red lights start flashing.

Worse, those responsible for program delivery sometimes have 'bonus blinkers' meaning that they try to deliver only what is in the official scope of the project and 'to hell with the rest of the organization' that might be adversely impacted by the project, directly or indirectly.

That's typically the way because that's the way they do things.

I can understand it. If you've been a program management professional for 20 years and never dealt with risk in the way I'm suggesting, then why would you feel the need to start to now - especially if I'm not around to prompt you and nobody else who looks at the program (including internal audit) say anything? If everyone seems okay with patchy and unimaginative risk information in some neglected section at the back of program update packs, then why would you want to stir up a hornets' nest?

I understand why they typically do it the way they do but the thing is, the consideration of risk in major programs could be far more insightful which would help better risk taking and increase the confidence of successful delivery of the program and the broader success of the business (beyond the program).

It's amazing how much of a breakthrough it can be to switch to a program management approach which requires workstreams to estimate the probability of tasks being achieved on time. The acknowledgement that confidence must surely be less than 100% enables more mature conversation on uncertainty and risk than an assertion that everything is absolutely fine and there is 100% confidence of successful delivery. There is certainly irony in the fact that program steering boards and others take confidence from those expressing 100% confidence in delivery because how can people be that certain?

The logic for improved consideration of risk in programs seems strong so the challenge is probably more about achieving behavioural change than it is explaining the logic.

There are of course a multitude of well-established behavioural change techniques around which could be adapted and adopted for use in particular organisations. There is also an opportunity to improve the training of program management professionals to lessen the grip of previous ways of doing things.

The next time you pick up a program update deck, take a look at how risk and uncertainty is being addressed and try to work out how mature you think the conversation is likely to be about probabilities of success. Take care in how you try to improve things because remember you will more than likely be up against years of different practice... people don't like change.

If you use all five lasers though, I'm pretty sure they will help you see, how shall I say it... room for improvement.

I think the risk management lessons to highlight from this chapter come from both the article itself and the background story about the show and I'd say they include:
- 'Plan C' might end up being best of all but you might need a miracle for that to be the case so don't count on it
- Thing sometimes go a bit (quite a lot) faster than you were expecting so be ready to go!
- Change programs typically only address a subset of the changes in riskiness that they bring
- Program management might have been done that way across the market for 20 years but

improvements opportunities can be very obvious if you have the right mindset
- Bringing about improved program management is more about methods for behavioural change than it is explanation of logic

15

TEN THINGS YOUR BUSINESS SHOULD HAVE BUT POSSIBLY DOESN'T (YET)

LinkedIn article:

PART A

The list might run to more than ten items but here is the first batch. I think the points are industry agnostic and are likely to be applied in a variety of ways in different companies but I believe many firms don't yet have them, despite the logic for them being strong.

1. The ability to demonstrate a cohesive risk management approach to shareholders and/or other stakeholders
2. A business strategy map which contains appropriate risk management activity linked directly to each component of the map
3. An explicit approach to managing people risk which formally acknowledges the way in which effective people risk management underpins all other forms of risk management activity
4. Measures of risk management agility and risk capability transition plans for an increasingly digital world
5. Access to a team of risk management professionals who move from point to point in an organization to help troubleshoot and deal with particular risk management challenges

PART B

Hello progress fans. Here's Part B of the list... this time centred around risk aspects of change and major programs. Let me know what you think. As before, I think the points are industry agnostic and are likely to be applied in a variety of ways in different companies but I believe many firms don't yet have them, despite the logic for them being strong:

6. A standardized way of ensuring all change programs include proper consideration and appropriate use of behavioural change techniques during planning and execution

7. An approach to optimizing risk management effectiveness which can cope with the interactions between the risk management framework, those using it and the different way it is used in underlying business processes

8. A program management methodology which properly addresses risks to, in and of the program, not just "in"

9. Clear accountabilities and responsibilities for managing risk... in particular, the ability to spot conflicts of interest and possible conflicts on roles such as; risk taking, helping others take risk, stopping others taking risk, keeping score of others' risks and, independent review of risk management

10. Good understanding of how you and your risk management capability is perceived by others

What else would you add?

In case you were wondering, I published this piece in two separate posts because I was experimenting with whether articles or posts got the greatest number of views (turns out it is the latter). The trouble with posts is that there is a limit on character numbers you can include in them so that was one reason for splitting it into two sections.

The other reason was to see if one half of the list flew faster than the other (it didn't).

The article is pretty self-explanatory when it comes to what is meant by each item in the lists so I won't go into them here - especially as many of them are covered in more detail in other articles described in the book.

I think the interesting thing for you and me to consider right now is not what each item on the lists mean but why they are on the lists at all.

Look at the items on the list again, they are not too wacky, are they? Each of them seems perfectly reasonable and sound perfectly achievable (you would think). As the text points out, the logic for each of them is pretty strong and most (if not all) are industry agnostic.

And we don't have idiots running our businesses so why is it you will not see these things in place as often as you might think?

Use the lists as a checklist for your own organization and see how you get on. I'll be amazed if you've got all of them nailed.

Welcome to the world of risk management, my friend. A place where there is so much opportunity for progress it is seems almost unreal.

Like other areas of possible progress, chucking the list over the wall and expecting people to get on with it won't work. Shouting at them to do it might work in some instances but is unlikely to be a reliable strategy for the longer term. Smarter behavioural change techniques need to be used even to get people to do what is logical.

Keep this list tucked away somewhere safe. The next time someone tries to tell you how good risk management is in their organization and you feel the need to challenge, take the list out, buff it up, and make some enquiries about how they are getting on with each of them.
Be ready for the usual excuses. Remember though, it can be okay not to have these things (most organisations are allowed to be risky and have sub-optimal risk management if they wish) but as per other articles in this book, those who don't should be ready for

a mature conversation with stakeholders about why they've chosen not to.

'We didn't know it was a thing' is surely behind us nowadays!

Although each of the items on the list could be tip in themselves, I think the main points to be summarised are:

- A lot of logically sound risk management features are not in place in many organisations
- It's hard to work out 'why?'
- Be ready to ask/answer the question

16

MIRROR, MIRROR ON THE WALL...

LinkedIn article:

Take a good look in the mirror. Okay, we know it's a reflection therefore not a completely accurate representation of what others see when they look at you but it's not bad. It helps a lot with self-awareness. You might even take some action as a result of looking in the mirror.

Great!

Does the mirror tell you what others see when they look at you? Well, yes - sort of. Does it tell you what they feel about you? Probably less so.

If only we could see ourselves through the eyes of others – and understand how we come across to them.

We might take different action as a result.

What's the corporate equivalent of looking in the mirror? We are interested in how we come across to customers and other stakeholders so we can take action. Anything which helps us see things "through their eyes" should be helpful (subject to cost).

What about risk management functions? Who are their "customers" and how are they perceived by them. How might they see themselves through the eyes of others and take appropriate action as a result? That's what the "Inside Out" service is all about and I'd love to tell you more.

There you go - short and sweet and a shameless plug for a new service!

How very vulgar of me.

Before you go off in a huff though, let me explain a bit more about what lay behind this article and what is still one of the most underused "superpowers" in risk management.

Let's start with Robert Burns. That in itself is a novelty of course because things tend to end with Robert Burns.

Not sure who Robert Burns is? He's only the author of Auld Lang Syne! You know, the song people sing at New Year and, given this is a risk management book, it is worth mentioning that it was featured in the Poseidon Adventure.

Anyway, Robert Burns (A.K.A. Scotland's national bard), wrote lots of great stuff and one of my favourite quotes from him is as follows:

'O wad some Power the giftie gie us, to see oursels as ithers see us!'

...or in modern English...

'Oh would some Power the gift give us, to see ourselves as others see us'

The phrase comes from his poem 'To a louse' which is about the sighting of a louse in a pretentious woman's hair and Burns makes the point that we would be saved from many mistakes and foolish thoughts if only we could see ourselves through the eyes of others.

It really would be a superpower wouldn't it if we always understood accurately how we came across to others. Imagine what you could do armed with that information.

'There goes old Midas himself' people would whisper as you swaggered about convincing people to do what you wanted through the dark art of actually understanding how you came across.

Mirror, mirror on the wall (which was a reference to the fairy tale Snow White of course) was certainly an eye-catching heading for this short post.

I made the point that self-awareness is more than just looking in the mirror because sometimes you see what you want to see in a mirror. In my bathroom mirror at home, I am thinner and have thicker hair than in real life.

Sometimes it's good that the mirror doesn't voice its own opinion because Snow White gives us some clues as to what can happen if they do. I mean, if mirrors all started getting all sarcastic with us, our dwindling self-confidence would gone in a couple of shaving sessions!

Anyway, why was I drawing attention to self-awareness? Well I could see money being spent in organisations on how they come across to customers. Customer experience and marketing initiatives aimed at understanding and shaping others' views on the organization and its profits were plentiful although all subject to an economic limit of course. Those should be familiar to risk functions operating in those organisations, some of whom, for differing reasons, might well have been involved in certain aspects of the initiatives themselves.

Risk management specialists should therefore be familiar with the concept of understanding others' perceptions.

They also know that the views of others are also important when it comes to evaluating performance and the consideration of consequent remuneration arrangements. Everyone knows the boss' view of you is important - that's not lost on people.

What though of the perceptions of others about the risk specialists in organisations? Well, actually, I think this is also pretty well understood - at least at a high level and by that I mean risk management teams tend to know who their supporters are and who is less receptive to them.

Some might argue that the perceptions of others (apart from their boss) shouldn't really matter because they want to be challenging with a degree of independence etc.

I can understand that point of view. If the risk management department feels it has no responsibility or duty to influence those running the business other than as an independent assurance provider then so be it.

Although I haven't got the complete statistical set of all risk functions, I'm pretty sure that most don't think that way. Instead, they feel that they do have an obligation to help the business improve the management of risk. For them, perceptions of others is a critical aspect of exerting their desired level of influence.

So how might they gauge the opinion of others?

Well, there will be some obvious evidence already in existence. What do people state in emails to them? How well are they involved in key decisions? How do people react to request etc?

That is evidence of sorts, which can be used to understand the perceptions of others.

Can anything else be done?

For a minute, let's take a detour. I sometimes do a bit of coaching for up-and-coming stars in professional services. Like I did before them, they sometimes have hang-ups from previous experiences and are often a little paranoid about how they are perceived by others (which

I would say is a good thing). They are also frequently trying to work out how best to behave inside the organization in order to influence others.

For some, a good tip is to behave as though others in your organization are clients of your organization because 'If you treat those inside your organization as though they were clients, you might find yourself operating in a different way'.

It's amazing sometimes how it takes somebody to tell you something before you realise it... even though it seems obvious in retrospect. When people try this out, they frequently report that it gives them a new perspective.

Back to risk functions now. Do they treat internal stakeholders as though they are clients?

To a degree they will of course.

However, could a more insightful analysis of how others do or might perceive them lead to a more effective function? You betcha!

Imagine risk functions took the time to decompose everything they do and invested quality time in understanding how what they say or write and how they behave in certain situations influences others' perceptions of them.

What if they broke down their internal "customer" journeys in the same way that their broader organisation looks at its external customer journeys and, subject to an economic limit, used a customer experience type lens to dissect all the current interface points and work out how every single one of them could be improved in a technical, process and behavioural way?

Imagine if a risk function's development plan was comparable to the development plan of an up and coming partner in a Big 4 consulting firm?

Most risk functions do have an idea of what they want to improve and might have some ideas as to how they might set about doing that over the weeks and months which follow. While such a high level "plan" might be useful, the personal equivalent would have been way to generic for an ultimately successful would-be partner. Success is to be found in the detail... typically how you influence over and above technical competence or logical righteousness.

Maybe one day risk functions will actually do this as part of their annual planning and more frequent adjustments to priorities. Perhaps they will do it in a proper way, being open to attitudinal and behavioural improvement ideas alongside an internal customer experience proposition that the externally facing CX (Customer Experience) guys would be proud of.

The risk management learning from this article is:
1) Use customer experience techniques to understand how risk functions come across to others inside their business, and to shape smart improvement actions as a result.

17

JOHN BERCOW - "Ordeeeeeeeerrrrrr.
Orrrrrrrrdeeeeeeeerrrrr!"

There weren't that many Conservative voters in the town I grew up in. Very few. It was probably to do with the coal mines and steel works and the prevailing local perception of Margaret Thatcher's role in their decline.

It must have been difficult being the Tory candidate there in those days... knocking on door after door, mustering up a big smile only for the door to be shut in your face time after time when the householder spotted the big blue rosette. If you were also English then (rather unfairly) it significantly reduced your chances of getting beyond "Good evening, I'm John Bercow and your local Conservative candidate. Have you worked out which way you are going to vo..." SLAM!

Bing-bong!

I was in the house alone so opened the front door and looked down the steep stairs to the bottom where a cheery looking smiley chap said " Good evening, I'm John Bercow..." you know how it goes so I don't need to fill in the rest of his introduction.

"Well yes, actually I have worked out which way I'm going to vote" I said bursting with pride that I was on top of the politics for the first General Election that I'd been old enough to vote in.

"And may I ask whether you would consider voting for me?" he asked with what must have been all the expectancy of an old car tyre.

I can't say for sure but I'm pretty certain he went to turn on his heels and leg it down the path but seemed to do a double take when I said; "You. I'm going to vote for you".

He was clearly delighted and we had a high energy chat for about 20 mins which was nice of him, really although he probably had few better things to do that night (because the result of the election locally was always going to be a forgone conclusion).

I can't really remember what we talked about. It was before my meeting with Jeffrey Archer (yes, that's right, my meeting with Jeffrey Archer - not John Bercow - and I'm keeping the Jeffrey Archer story for another volume!) so we definitely didn't talk about that. I can only remember that I liked him, he seemed to like me and we both were going to vote for the same person at the general election and were in the wrong place to be voting that way. It's funny how your vote sometimes doesn't seem to matter in a democracy.

We both moved to London after that... not together of course... no gossip there. We both moved separately.

To be fair, I'm not sure he had ever really moved to his would-be constituency so was probably just returning home and I imagine he made the journey in some top-of-the-range yuppie style BMW convertible... along the lines of the one I'd stared at in a car showroom window every day on the way to university. I made the one-way journey to London on an overnight National Express bus which took some incomprehensible detours to pick up and drop of other hooded passengers on the winding nigh-time journey to the great metropolis.

I could at least take comfort in the fact that as School Captain and Conservative candidate in the school mock general election, I'd secured 1% more of the vote than John Bercow had in the real general election. That was of small consolation though as the reality was we'd both taken an absolute drubbing. We were beaten hands-down by local favourites, Labour, and it was interesting to note that in the years which followed, Labour lost out to a different party. Time changes everything.

He went on to do big things and as a high profile Speaker of the House of Commons for many years had an impressive impact on the work of democracy in our country - famously climaxing in presiding over the Brexit shenanigans - and although I have no way of knowing if some of the personal allegations about his working styles are true, the impression I got as a member of the public was that he was trying to ensure fairness in the House and that he did a first class job of that.

What then are my risk management tips from that doorstep encounter with John Bercow?

You have to do the grunt work before you get the glory.

It must have been hell for him to be the candidate at the time but it was all part of his development journey to greatness.

Like all graduates who were at the top end of academic performance in their year, I burst onto the work scene like on over-confident foal. Looking back, I can characterize some of it with the question "Right, what decisions do you want me to make?" as that was the sort of thing that I could well have muttered given my mindset.

In subsequent years, I noticed it in other bright young things too. Of course, the only real decision you want them to make at that stage is whether to go to Starbucks or Café Nero but yours is definitely a flat white, thanks very much.

Okay so I am exaggerating a little with that. Of course there are other more work-focused decisions that you can and do let your junior workforce make and take (by the way I see 'make' and 'take' as two distinct stages -

especially in relation to decisions on managing risks... that was something else I got from the early years with Professor Dickson).

Anyway, my point is that whatever your inherent capability, you usually need to do all the grunt work before you get to the opportunity for the glory.

My tennis coach is hot on this. When he observes me playing with others in a doubles match he loves it when someone hits a winning smash from close to the net because it give him a chance to air one of his most well-known sayings; "Nice shot but you only had that chance because your partner did all the grunt work!".

He is right about that but it's interesting how you can sometimes forget it. When you move your feet and move your feet and move your feet again to line up a smash which goes like a bullet and bounces just inside the baseline before rocketing off beyond your opponent it is such a fantastic feeling that you can't help but raise your hand to the appreciative crowd (usually just a pigeon) and totally forget about the massive slog your playing partner just put in to press your opposition into giving you that 'sitter'.

By the way, another of my coach's favourite sayings is "Play percentage... no winners!". By that he usually means don't take a chance by hitting it really hard because in the long run you are likely to be less successful than you will be if you hit it more reliably and force your opponent into having to play it back again etc. Everyone wants to hit a winner of course but at the lower end of the amateur game (which is where I play), percentages seem to hold the key to victory. There are risk management lessons in that as well of course but I'm getting distracted!

Where were we? Oh yes, you need to put in the grunt before you get the glory. People who work their way up through the ranks in highly competitive organisations, as

I did, will tell you that because they put in a shift alright. It's not just about the work of course, it's dealing with everything else that you need to address to be successful too.

That was probably what took John Bercow up north. On the first day he joined the Tories, I can't imagine he was welcomed with open arms by the party chairman saying "At long last, please come in you majestic individual... we've been waiting so long for someone like you to join us - please have a safe seat in a lovely constituency and become Speaker of the House"!

I think his journey to the top was tougher than that and if it meant putting in some grunt over the border then so be it.

One of the downsides of working with great people is that they are all pretty good and although that can make the team highly competitive in the market, it can make competition inside the team even tougher. Just look at how unhappy some of the best footballers in the world get when they lose out to fierce competition inside their team.

Hard work, sacrifice and effort is needed to get the shot at glory.

Specifically in relation to risk management, this can often arise in relation to decisions being made taking into account input from line management and/or risk functions about risk levels and possible control actions.

Being right about risk is the easy bit. It's relatively easy to say "I think we should do this because..." or "I don't think you should do this because..."

A battle of the self-righteous can be fought with logic alone but such showdowns are a pretty high-risk tactic, aren't they? Board meetings and sub committees such as the Board Risk Committee and Board Audit

Committee are sometimes the scene of such clashes but more typically the issues are raised and resolved beforehand and in "offline" situations. That is one of those things which is not obvious until someone tells you about it.

It's the effort involved in getting to the stakeholders beforehand and influencing what they do and what they say beforehand which can be the secret to effective Board committee meetings - people putting in the grunt beforehand.

Of course, more effort is needed in the first instance to research and shape your proposition in the first place before you can take it to anyone.

So if you want to make an impact on the management of risk you need to put the grunt in to secure a senior position and then put more grunt in on a daily basis to lay the ground work for glory moments (which should never be schadenfreudian although it is an unfortunate truth in risk management that they sometimes are).

Of course, even at a late stage, requests for further risk analysis under different scenarios etc might need to be dealt with. More grunt needed.

Is the improvement of risk management therefore more grunt than glory? I think it is.

Little people grow

This is not a cheap shot about John Bercow's height as I wouldn't do that (woops too late).

People tend to be familiar with the concept of a chain only being as strong as its weakest link and there is no shortage of case studies on relatively junior individuals being the cause of some very significant and in many cases tragic risk events.

While that is an important risk management lesson, it's not the one I wanted to focus on in relation to my encounter with John.

Neither is it to do with the well-known phrase of "Be nice to people on the way up because you will see them again on the way down". I understand the sentiment in that message but it belongs more to a time when people were loyal to organisations who were loyal to them in return and I'm not sure that is the way anymore. For example, the shift away from final salary pensions to defined contribution pensions shifts so much risk back onto individuals as do other contractual changes such as the move to zero hours contracts etc. There is probably still some truth in the statement but if the reality is that you won't see them again on the way down because you will simply be jettisoned then perhaps a better saying would be "Be nice to people on the way up because you will at least have a clear conscience".

Anyway, that's another matter, dear reader, and 'conscience credits' is a concept I've written a short play about so definitely one for another day!

The point I want to make in this book is more to do with what influences the behaviour of future leaders. Some of the junior people being asked to undertake the most unrewarding/ thankless tasks can end up being the ones exerting quite a significant influence on the direction of our countries or organisations.

Early exposure to risk taking behaviour probably has an influence on how one operates. Certainly, observations on the culture inside certain types of financial institutions at certain points in our history (such as those characterized in the movie "The Wolf of Wall Street") make it difficult to feel comfortable about that behaviour in retrospect but the apparent tolerance (and even endorsement) of it at the time probably resulted in shaping the thoughts and actions of the next generation in ways that society might not otherwise see as beneficial.

Monkey see, monkey do.

The trouble with risk is that it can have upside and downside. Bad risk taking can result in significant gain. Those learning from and emulating bad risk taking can end up winners. Conversely, good risk taking can result in significant loss.

Machiavellian ethics and good risk taking are not always happy bedfellows... except in the long run.

Maybe this is why risk management education is so important. Would gambling be less of a problem and more of a source of fun if people understood more about how to understand and manage the upside and downside risks involved?

Could we create a generation of informed, good risk takers instead of a mix of ignorant lucky and ignorant unlucky risk takers?

The great thing about good risk taking is the logic is so very strong... but right now only a small minority ever benefit from quality risk management education.

As the song from Les Miserables (one of my favourite musicals) goes "Be careful as you go, 'cause little people grow". That song emphasizes the threat from little people growing up very nicely. However, it is the good risk-taking opportunity to be gained from little people growing up educated in risk management which motivates me.

I really hope that some of those people will learn something from my experiences shared in this book. If you are one of them with an appetite for learning about risk management then whatever your age, religion, gender, sexual orientation and wherever you sit on the ranges of diversity which make humans so great, go for it guys! Grow well in a risk management sense and be great at good risk taking!

18

LinkedIn article:

I'll keep this short as we are in the middle of a crisis.

What are your future scouts telling you about what else is important right now?

Whatever phase of the crisis and recovery you are in, it's worth enabling at least some people to consider the future unencumbered by the day-to-day immediate pressures.

The concept of freeing up some staff ("future scouts") to focus on the medium and long- term options and opportunities for your business is easy enough to understand... even for those who haven't done it yet. In practical terms though, what would they do? After all, it had better be good because otherwise I'm sure they would be very useful firefighting short-term issues.

Two things:

1. They clear the path ahead so that when you get there, some things have already been done and it is easier for you to continue on your journey at pace. For example, options and opportunities under different scenarios will have been clarified and articulated with some necessary actions already planned for different possible routes

2. They help us make sure that in our short term "panic", we don't forget about all the things we know (or may come to realize) are critical for our future success and we have to give at least some

time and attention to today. In other words, all
the key items on our strategy map

If you have a good strategy map, you will already know
what all those things are. If you don't then your future
scouts can maybe create one quickly to help with speedy
feedback on everything that is important today for
medium and longer-term success.

---

*...in the future, what additional
things will we be proud to say that
we did in the midst of chaos which
actually sowed the seeds of longer
term success?*

Of course, our strategic goals might be changing. The
items on our strategy map might be changing in relative
importance as a result. For example, doing more to truly
understand customer needs might now be increasing in
importance on strategy maps because of the possible
dynamics we will witness as we come through and out of
this crisis. Maybe some new items will appear on
strategy maps.

The items on the strategy maps might therefore need to
be calibrated and adjusted but we can make those
decisions consciously based on emerging truths about
future scenarios and we can make sure we don't forget
about things which don't seem important now in the heat
of individual "battles" but will turn out to have been
critical in winning the "war".

Put it another way... in the future, when history shows
that our organization was successful, what additional
things will we be proud to say that we did in the midst of

chaos which actually sowed the seeds of longer term success?

> *...don't forget about things in the heat of individual "battles" which will turn out to have been critical in winning the "war".*

Of course, without short-term survival there is no medium or longer-terms but spending some time now on medium and longer-term issues and working out the implications of those for current activity should improve the likelihood and magnitude of success for those that do survive.

Fire-fighters don't have a problem keeping busy in most organisations. There is usually lots to do - especially in the middle of a crisis.

'All hands to the pump' was an order for everyone on a ship to pump water out if it was sinking and is a phrase that most people are familiar with. There was a lot of that going on during the crisis and at the time of writing there still is.

It's understandable, isn't it?

Even at times when there is no such broader crisis facing humanity, the focus on short term can be deemed extremely important. For example, listed companies who need to report their earnings on say a quarterly basis sometimes find it difficult to look beyond the next reporting date - especially if there are significant bonus arrangements in play for senior executives which are tied to those short-term performance figures.

Some companies have taken quite a few steps to encourage interest in longer term results by amending remuneration arrangements with clawbacks and other types of device designed to try and ensure that short term success is not at the expense of longer-term success or even survival.

Even in non-listed companies, there is a tension between the short and longer terms it's just that the numbers aren't always so public so there is a reduced risk of immature evaluation of risk and performance management by third party investors. That means there can sometimes be a little more breathing space.

Whatever the length of the temporal dimensions, the point is the same - keep an eye on the future when you are dealing with all the issues of the moment. If you don't believe me, then ask Michael J Fox or, probably better, Doc from Back to the Future fame!

Humour aside, I'm right, aren't I?

Smart risk management thinking and action in organisations during crises will certainly address the immediate challenges but it should also be adding value to the activity needed to secure future success too so in the same way as the article suggests some resource is released from 'the pump' in order to look at the future, risk management activity should follow suite too.

In summary, I think the two main risk management tips from this chapter are probably as follows:
- The likelihood and magnitude of future success for those who survive the crisis is likely to be affected by what is done now for the benefit of the longer term.
- Effective risk management should be as much about supporting/ ensuring future scouting than surrounding 'all hands on the pump'.

19

CLARIFYING RESPONSIBILITY IN DIGITAL CHANGES AND MORE DECENTRALIZED DECISION MAKING

LinkedIn article:

The big changes happening around us provide opportunity for a better way of clarifying responsibility.

One of the first letters to an editor I wrote was in 1990 or 1991 and it was to Paul Bawcutt who was the editor of a risk management journal called "Foresight". It was on the subject of whether risk managers should have direct responsibility for managing risk or not. There were different views around at the time and there still are today. A quarter of a century has passed and the debate over the roles of risk functions and others involved in managing risk still rages on.

...despite guidance, standards and regulations, we are not agreed.

Despite guidance, standards and regulations, we are not agreed. Even inside some industries with prescriptive rules around the topic and within geographic areas, differences in views and application remain.

The internet is rife with disgruntlement on generic approaches which just don't seem to work for all people and companies, all of the time. When I talk to Chief Risk Officers, they are often frustrated by the the current state and a couple have called "Emperor's New Clothes" on some of the high profile would-be solutions such as the

"1.5 Line of Defence" which is getting a lot of airtime in banking. I've written in the past about the issues and don't feel the need to repeat them here.

I think I might be coming to a conclusion on this topic. Certainly, 25+ years is a long time to have thought about it so maybe a conclusion is due and it is as follows:

Don't look for generic, universally agreed, statements of responsibility for risk to adopt in your organization. If you think you've found one – don't use it, blindly.

Ones which might appear at first to be "universally" accepted, typically don't stand up if you look closely enough. Even descriptions coming from regulators can be loaded with ambiguity and/or implemented inconsistently and therefore cannot be relied upon to provide the clarity which should be useful to those organizations trying to manage risk in structured way. History shows us that.

So what should we do, then?

Hmm… well at the risk of sounding a bit obvious to some and inflammatory to others, I'd say it's important for firms to devise their own descriptions. Yes, they might still have to ultimately translate back into more primitive language if regulators and others struggle to cope with something they are not used to but the most important thing is to achieve clarity that works for the firm, isn't it?

"Double hmmn". Let me be clear, I'm not suggesting firms should drop everything they currently have on responsibilities and start again. While that might be productive in the long run, it could be a recipe for chaos in the short term so it's probably not a good option!

...the most important thing is to achieve clarity that works for the firm, isn't it?

Let's take two examples of big change happening currently where something better could emerge, though:

1. **Digital changes.** The world is changing and the move to digital is bringing shifts to the way organizations operate and who has responsibility within them. For most, certainly beyond the short term, digital is not a standalone thing. Instead, it impacts other processes, departments and functions. Time is being, and will be, spent clarifying who is responsible and for what in the new world.
2. **Decentralised decision making.** Decentralization of decision making through edge technology, artificial intelligence and more empowered and collaborative small businesses means that thought will be given as to how these decisions should be made and who (and increasingly "what") will make those decisions.

These two examples will be happening now, or in the near future, in a great many organizations around the world. That means there is now a superb opportunity to clarify responsibility for risk management in and around those decisions. Both are "new world" situations so where better to come up with a new way of clarifying responsibility and accountability than there?

How might it actually be done in those situations, though?

There are options.

Rich scenarios can be used to clarify or stress test responsibilities and accountabilities so using such an approach seems sensible. It is also a good way to help everyone become familiar with the peculiarities of the new world we are all entering into.

...become familiar with the peculiarities of the new world we are all entering into.

Inside each scenario there will be a need to describe the actions and responsibilities of individuals and/or functions and this presents a risk of slipping into old habits. Instead, new but logically sound, terminology can help. One such set of terminology can be found in the "Risk Management Formations" approach where individuals'/ functions' responsibilities are clarified for specific situations using one or more than one of the Take/Help/Stop/KeepScore/Independent, risk management purpose angles.

Life would be easier for everyone if we had a common and truly universally accepted set of descriptions for risk and accountability which was consistently implemented in the same way, everywhere.

However, we don't have it and I'm not sure we should spend more than 25 years trying to find it. Instead, we could perhaps move on and, regulators and others permitting, use smart and clever ways to get real clarity

> on responsibilities for managing risk in our changing world.
>
> It seems to be within our reach but we each need to grasp it for ourselves.

Just before the pandemic really hit the UK, I had confirmed my willingness to continue as organizer of the grounds maintenance rota at my tennis club.

It seemed a pretty clear role to me - organize the rota for grounds maintenance showing who was due to cut the grass etc each week, tell them if anything in particular needed attention to and then just record that they had done it.

What could be clearer than that?

I checked the previous year's records and set up the maintenance rota for the year ahead - all "good to go".

Sure enough it did go and carried on flying out the window when the virus hit!

In those very early days of lockdown in the UK, there was a lot of fear and anxiety about the direct health impact of the virus itself. Later, concern extended to the indirect health and current and future financial impact of the deadly visitor but at the time is was all about everyone being worried they would catch it.

In an effort to do the right thing and prevent the spread of the virus at our club we suspended the grounds maintenance rota because we felt that sharing the tools and accessing the buildings etc could spread the risk. This was no attempt at bravado. It's just that it was easier to ask people to stay away than it was to coordinate controlled entrance/exit and the use of disinfected tools etc.

Now the thing is, there is a lot of grass at our tennis club and it grows like you wouldn't believe in the springtime. I therefore had a choice to make. I could either:

    a)   Stay away and let the grass grow into what would appear at first to be a beautiful wild-flower meadow but would quickly evolve into a weed-ridden jungle

...or...

    b)   Cut it myself

I decided to go for (b)... after all, lockdown might only last a few weeks and it would be a nice bit of exercise given that the gyms were closed and we were not allowed to go anywhere.

Also, who else should do it? If the person doing the rota cannot or chooses not to find people to do the work then surely he needs to do it himself? Looking back, the definition of responsibility had perhaps not been so clear after all and this unexpected event (the pandemic) had shed light on some significant ambiguity that I had found myself at the sharp end of.

Due to a malfunctioning lawnmower (which with my tennis club members are only too familiar) it took about 2.5hrs to cut the grass in each of weeks one and two. Then there was weedkiller to lay down on and around the courts. Then there was... well, you get the picture.

Nevertheless, with a spring in my step and my trusty noise-cancelling Bose headphones secured over the top of my baseball cap, I put on my sunglasses and got on with it to a soundtrack of Bluegrass from a Spotify playlist. In those early weeks of pandemic naivety I found the discovery of this musical genre to be most conducive to working on the land in the hot sunshine (for we were starting a prolonged period of sunny weather).

Over the weeks, as the ground dried and the dust started to kick up, the novelty wore off but I still quite enjoyed the exercise and the tangible results you get from gardening.

However, it began to dawn on everyone that we were in this for the long haul and that meant me carrying on with performing the grounds maintenance duties myself.

To be honest, it wasn't really a chore. I had managed to get the weekly grass cut down to only two hours because the mower wasn't playing up anymore and exercise opportunities remained in short supply for much of the lockdown. In the end I did it for four months when we all felt comfortable enough to resume the rota under clarified social distancing rules etc.

The consequences of unclear responsibilities can, of course, be far more significant in business circles and far more painful for anyone who finds themselves suffering when an ambiguity, or an error/ omission, has come to light.

If there was a giant pie chart showing the internet airtime that individual risk management topics get, I'm pretty sure that the big bright orange responsibilities and accountabilities segment would be dazzling us all.

Goodness me, it doesn't half get a lot of commentary. Whether it is all about the Three Lines (of Defence) or regulatory attempts at generating clarity through job titles, or whether it is as basic as the role of the Chief Risk Officer, the arguments about who is responsible for what in the world of risk management rages on.

On the one hand, you might think that means it must be important. You'd be right.

On the other hand, you might think it can't be that important because otherwise it would have been resolved by now. Hmm, I don't think that is quite correct.

I can think of quite a few other things which divide people on our planet but have not yet been resolved. Can you?

In a long published article I wrote for the EY Journal of Financial Perspectives with the help of some very bright people, I went into detail about the problems with the three lines of defence and suggested a better way of clarifying accountability using language which had not yet been contaminated or distorted by inconsistent application in different organisations.

One of the problems is people can be stuck in their ways and once they have something in their heads about risk management accountability, it can be difficult to get them to see things from another angle - especially when the stakes can be high and regulators show little appetite for anything different to that which they are used to... even if the prevailing methods don't work particularly well.

It seemed to me that if it proved difficult to get people to be open to new ideas (even if they are better than the status quo) then a good place to try it would be where and when there is underlying business change.

Digital changes and decentralized decision making were two such areas that I highlighted in the article. As responsibilities would need to be reset anyway, why not take the opportunity to do it in a smarter way?

What was/is a smarter way? I mean it's always easy to knock something but unless you can come up with something better then it doesn't really help all that much to be critical.

Step up Risk Management Formations!

'Risk management what?' I hear you ask, dear reader. 'Tell me more of this thing you speak of' I hear you holler.

Nothing's getting past you now, my friend, is it?

Risk Management Formations. It is (drum roll) the best and most original alternative to "three lines" way of allocating risk management responsibility (crashing cymbal)! Risk management's equivalent of the best thing since sliced bread (another cymbal crash)!

Yes, ladies and gentlemen, roll up, roll up for risk management's miracle elixir. The thing you've all been waiting for your entire risk management lives.

Don't be shy now, come on, step forward to be enlightened and empowered beyond your wildest dreams because never in the history of mankind has there been such a dazzling breakthrough in expressions of risk management accountability.

Let's be having you. Who's first then?

Come on, someone has to be first, don't they?

Anyone?

Hello?

That was pretty much the journey I went on with Risk Management Formations.

I still think it was brilliant - creatively devised and then worked through in detail to ensure its practicability and even it's 'backwards compatibility' with Three Lines and UK Senior Managers Regime language.

Deep down, I really hope that one day, people will see the light on this and it will become the standard way of defining responsibility for risk in individual situations... because it's at that level of granularity that clarity lies - not the big sweeping generalisations that are nearly always currently used and don't even work well for simple structures like football teams (as the original article in the journal points out).

After I left EY, there were a few clients of mine who really loved Risk Management Formations and used it to clarify the basis for risk-related inputs to bonus and remuneration arrangements. Those who took the trouble to read the article and understand the approach, tended to like it.

Of course, most people were either unaware of it or felt that their existing approach meant that, for whatever reason, they didn't need to consider this alternative. I have never pushed it hard into the marketplace and maybe that's what I should get around to doing sometime. Certainly, if investors or other stakeholders wanted to see clearer accountability for risk in organisations it might hasten my go-to-market tactics on this.

In the meantime, here is my simple plea... whenever you use future scenarios to stress test risk related responsibilities and accountabilities (and please do use scenarios otherwise we are back to square one) in a new or changing part of your organisation, please take the opportunity to set real clarity by using Risk Management Formations or if you've found something better then use that.

Thinking about the tips from this chapter, they are possibly best summarised as follows:
- Although it arguably needs to, the world doesn't want to change the way it currently describes responsibilities for risk - even though the prevailing methods are full of ambiguity
- Better methods like Risk Management Formations exist and are useful to those who take the time to understand them
- Deal with the reluctance to change approaches by targeting areas of underlying business change such as digital changes or decentralized decision making

20

LinkedIn article:

Hello progress fans!

No, I haven't misspelled it... I mean the sound that an old-fashioned clock makes rather than the name of a well-known app.

It's actually quite interesting that for many, the words "tick tock" no longer look correct because they have become so familiar with the name of the app which I am not going to spell out although if I was a betting man, I'd reckon you would be able to guess it!

Anyway, tick tock it is, at least for the purposes of this article.

It's amazing how so many of us put up with mediocre, isn't it? Whether it is 'okay' speed and reliability from our internet service providers, 'okay' renewal service from insurance providers, 'okay' drying performance from dishwashers, 'okay' train punctuality or 'okay' table service in a restaurant, many of us are prone to being tolerant of the mediocre.

...especially in countries where people don't like to make a fuss - no names needed there methinks!

When something as big as this pandemic happens, many of us will be forced to accept more of the mediocre because options dry up, don't they?

When it comes to the management of risk in business though, the situation looks different.

...riskiness has increased in relative terms

For many firms, their riskiness has increased in relative terms (whatever the absolute level happens to be) because of the uncertainty inside and outside of their construct. The top line and the bottom line have increased upside and downside uncertainty about them even if the initial effect of the virus has been positive.

Staff numbers are changing too - sometimes because of the need to cut costs and sometimes because of other changing needs of the business.

All this change affects those with formal or informal, direct or indirect responsibility for risk management.

The opportunity stems from being able to take a step back and take stock of everything

---

For those with decision-making responsibility about the design and performance of risk management in firms, there is an opportunity emerging beyond the immediate chaos and heightened anxiety (positive or otherwise). The opportunity stems from being able to take a step back and take stock of everything important.

As part of that, there is the chance to fix things you haven't previously got around to. Fate is proving a platform for inorganic shifts.

One such possibility relates to grappling with mediocre approaches to risk management. Whether it is the people involved, the tools/frameworks they use, or the way in which they are adapted for use by those people in different organizational situations, now could be a good time to shake up things.

Fate is providing a platform for inorganic shifts

Why don't you have what you want? Maybe you want poor or mediocre risk management capability - there is nothing wrong with that as long as stakeholders are clear on your approach and you are prepared for the consequences. That hasn't changed although perhaps going forward stakeholders will be more scrutinous of risk management capability and effectiveness than they have been in the past (but that is the subject of another of my articles).

Maybe the recent experience and heightened riskiness going forward makes you less prepared to tolerate mediocrity though when it comes to the management of risk?

If so, do something about it. There possibly is, or will shortly be, availability of management talent like never before in many countries. Also, for those roles where geographic location has been proven to be relatively unimportant because of the increased realization of the benefits of remote working, top talent previously confined to the biggest cities can be accessed from anywhere (which is a reverse way of presenting the remote working case and one which seems to have received relatively little attention up until now).

Much of the available talent will be mediocre, though. You might even be forced into recruiting it because a regulator thinks it more important to have someone who has done that role before (even if he/she is mediocre) than it is to have a more capable person who is very familiar with the subject matter (but had never actually done the role before).

The thing is, some of the talent will not be mediocre but will instead be on the right side of it and, for a multitude of reasons, there is likely to be more of the better-than-mediocre talent available for work… at least in the short term, which is why timing is important.

It is becoming temporarily easier to replace mediocre talent in your organization, or in your advisor organisations (even if they work for a big branded consultancy) with better capability.

…[the opportunity] is to improve risk management by replacing mediocre

> *talent with that of better quality*
> _____
>
> I know there are lots of considerations around the evolution of workforces (and extended workforces) and some regulation governing what you can and cannot do and those need to be respected.
>
> Remember though, there is an opportunity right now which might not return for a generation. It is to improve risk management by replacing mediocre talent with that of better quality.
>
> Now is your chance – take it!

This article is both bleakly pessimistic and wonderfully optimistic at the same time, isn't it?

On the one hand, Doctor Death has arrived to deliver a digest of doom. On the other hand, a kind of Mary Poppins figure is not holding back in telling us that opportunity knocks and "is not a lengthy visitor" as someone once said.

If you were reading between the lines, you might also detect a hint of frustration in the text. If you are cynical then one of the things going through your mind could also be that there is a hint of salesmanship going on too. If you are a risk management specialist you are possibly wondering why I'm picking on your lot and if you are in management more generally then maybe you think it is about the risk management capability in line management.

I did realise when I was writing the article that it can be the sort of thing which runs the risk of turning people off.

166

'The word mediocre tends to imply some degree of majority and if you are implying that the majority are mediocre then you can stop right there, Mr Martin... we strongly object to...'

You know... that sort of thing.
I still wrote it though and although I paused and took a deep breath before hitting the "post" button on LinkedIn, it felt like the right thing to do... even if 'going with The Force, I was'.

There is a fine line between being courageous and being stupid when it comes to these sort of change tactics. I'm very aware of that and hope that, at least on this occasion, my aims and methods will be perceived as reasonable and justifiable by good, honest people of the parish.

Remember, the article was the latest action in my deep desire to bring about the sorts of changes in risk management that we can all be proud of. At EY, they used to say that an admirable goal for Partners was to "leave the Partnership in a better state than it was when you found it" and like some others, I have that as a goal when it comes to my life and risk management.

I sometimes imagine myself at the gates of heaven with some of the questioning going along the lines of;

"...and did you leave risk management on earth in a better state than you found it?"

'...well er, you see, that's quite a complicated thing to answer... I did this degree and then I went to London and.... '

Okay, I made that up - I've never imagined that heavenly scenario before but thought it would be a good way of explaining my feeling of purpose in relation to moving risk management forward.

It's that sense of purpose which makes me take risks sometimes in relation to articles (and internal communications). Nowadays, I try to avoid rushes of blood to the head and so tend to 'sleep on it' before publishing anything but behind all those self-control mechanisms that I've learnt and developed is this fundamental belief at my core which is that improved risk management would be good for us because the logic is so strong.

Some people are driven by the desire for humans to conquer inter-planetary travel and others by the wish to build the biggest structures on the planet. Some people want to change the world for social reasons and others want to protect it from environmental changes. Some are dreamers and some are pragmatists and both are needed for these challenges.

My drive comes from the recognition that improved risk management can help with all of these things.

I've also been smart enough to know that making progress on my goal means adopting a large dollop of style flexibility (if that's not an oxymoron). Different styles of communication are needed at different points in time so it's sensible to build your style flexibility kitbag to be able to work with that doctrine.

Like many things, it's obvious once somebody has told you it. Knowing that is therefore the easy bit. Making the judgements and consequent adjustments necessary is of course a much trickier thing to do which is why few master it (and I don't think I'm truly in that camp although I'd claim to have at least one foot in it).

Anyway, the point is, some of you will think I was stupid in writing this article and others will think I was courageous. There might also be others who think I was neither and don't understand what all the fuss was about... I was just drawing attention to a "once-in-a-lifetime opportunity" (which happened to be coming to a lot of people at the same time) to shake things up and at least recognize that top talent is available to replace the mediocre.

There is sometimes merit in discarding the "either/ors". There are moments when having to decide whether something is courageous or stupid is wasting energy.

They say 'Don't shoot the messenger', when confronted with an inconvenient truth... especially when the actual aim of the messenger is to point out an opportunity for you, and where he or she has made an effort to position the message in an acceptable way.

Blimey, I was getting a bit heavy there wasn't I? Right... the key learnings from this chapter are:

1) The pandemic has resulted in a (hopefully temporary) opportunity for a reshuffle of the best risk management talent across and between different organisations and geographies. Get what you want if it is not what you have.
2) Risk management mediocrity can exist separately or collectively in people, frameworks or the application of those frameworks to underlying business processes.
3) Don't shoot the risk management messenger
4) If you are the risk management messenger, think carefully about your communication style

21

RICHARD ATTENBOROUGH 'I just love biography, and I'm fascinated by people who have shifted our destinies or our points of views' and ALAN RICKMAN

I felt a tap on my shoulder so I turned around.

'Clive, let me introduce you to... Richard Attenborough'.

What do you think went on in my head? Was it:
  a) 'uh, okay then'
  b) 'who?'
  c) 'blimey it's Richard Attenborough!'

You are of course correct. It was indeed answer c because it was none other than 'Dickie" himself!

Fans of Jurassic Park, the Flight of the Phoenix, The Great Escape, Gandhi... (the list is almost endless) will know that the late Lord was true showbiz royalty so it really was a wonderful honour and experience to meet him.

As you might expect, he was charming, energetic and friendly and I have the photo of the two of us (well I wasn't going to let the photo opportunity pass now, was I?) as one of a few treasured photos in my study.

Other photos include me flying a plane above Stratford upon Avon, driving a Formula Ford racing car at Brands Hatch and standing inside Windsor Castle where I twice stayed for a few days... as you do!

In this last photo, I am part of a group of up-and-coming leaders that were brought together at Windsor Castle from a cross-section of British society to share leadership stories and learn from others. It was an amazing experience to be allowed to sit in one of the Knights of the Garter seats in St George's chapel during evensong.   In the same week it was also an amazing experience to wander back (slightly inebriated) from a local pub and scramble for our security passes as we approached the scariest security guards I have ever seen (apart from outside some nightclubs in my youth). It's amazing the sobering effect that a very serious looking hard-as-nails and highly trained soldier holding a machine gun has when you are walking straight towards him on a dark, balmy night!

More than anything though, that time at Windsor Castle helped me realise that despite my ambition, my desire to become a Partner at EY and my genuine passion for being part of the next generation of leaders of our society, the thing that was really, really important to me - above all else - was my wife and children. I am eternally grateful to all those involved in The Windsor Leadership Trust for helping me realise that truth... as well as all the other leadership learning which went along with it.

Anyway, as is often the case in this book, I digress.

Let's go back to the Savoy Hotel because that, dear reader, was where the conversations with Richard Attenborough and Alan Rickman happened. Oh, did I forget to mention Alan Rickman, earlier? I suppose it's easily done!

I'm kidding of course. Who would forget meeting Alan Rickman from Harry Potter, Sweeney Todd, Love Actually, Robin Hood... his list is almost endless, too.

It happened the same way with Alan as it did with Richard - a tap on the shoulder followed by; 'let me introduce you to... Alan Rickman'. I'll spare you the multiple-choice options on how I reacted to this one but let's just say my thoughts were roughly the same as when meeting Richard and leave it at that.

No really, I'm going to leave it at that and move on because I want to get back to the Richard Attenborough chat. I say 'chat' but the truth is I said very little because I didn't need to... he was so entertaining. The whole thing was over in a bit of a flash although it probably lasted for around ten minutes or so.

I could try and draw some risk management lessons from the discussion itself. I could also talk about how I was desperate to (but never did) meet Jonathan Pryce who was just over his shoulder.

However, I'm not going to do that. Instead, I'm going to pay tribute to this legend of showbiz by trying to be a bit more entertaining and draw on some of his films instead. Perhaps one of his best-known appearances is in relation to a couple of the Jurassic Park films. That's right, movies based around a theme park with real dinosaurs in it... what could possibly go wrong?

I'm going to avoid the obvious risk management lessons like 'dinosaurs will eat you if you try and feed them popcorn' or 'never be the one at the back on a ghost tour or a dinosaur trip' as the one at the back always gets picked off first.

I won't even succumb to the notion that building a theme park around live dinosaurs is a bad idea because that would be a lazy generalization and there are enough lazy statements made about avoiding opportunity because of risk. I'm all for taking the right sort of risks so if at some stage in the future a real one gets set up, I'm not ruling out supporting it in some form.

So, what less obvious lessons can I draw from those movies which might, just might, be helpful when we think about risk management in the real world?

Let's have a go with these ones, shall we?

Be creative and imaginative as you think about risk when creating a monster.

Figurative ones as well as actual ones. You know... figurative ones like those scary developments we build and have no real way of knowing for sure what it will lead to.

Yes folks, I mean the monsters of our digital age and 'well done if you got that at home' (as Richard Osman would say).

You see, I think you will need the creativity and imagination to anticipate risks to success and also to craft smart risk management activity.

Everyone knows that 2+2=4 but somewhere in our past, someone creative said it is possible to put 2+2 together and get 5. While a sure-fire route to failing school arithmetic exams, this holistic way of looking at things can also be a sure-fire route to business sales success which only goes to show how out of touch our educational system is with what is really useful in life!

Cost-cutting Doctor Deaths then jumped on the band wagon with the notion that you can put 2+2 together and get 3. Well done them... that is exactly what they usually ended up with (use your imagination to work out the different things that the numbers could mean and while you are at it, don't confuse cost cutting with value adding).

Anyway, one of the great things about big data is that it offers the potential to put 2+2 together and get 'x'. That might be 5 (or 3) but it might be something else altogether because combining previously separate things can have unexpectedly significant results.

Just think about those early apothecaries (and brewers for that matter), experimenting with previously unmixed potions. There they stood with their big boiling cauldron carefully pouring a smouldering liquid into another to see if it would make gold (in both senses of the word).

The lucky ones (and/or smart ones because in some situations it's hard to tell the difference, isn't it?) were rewarded with a glowing pot of treasure while the unlucky (or stupid... again, hard to tell the difference sometimes) ones had the top of their heads blown off!

I should maybe have warned you about the violent end to that last paragraph but we've already mentioned being eaten by dinosaurs in this chapter so I think it is reasonable to assume that you were already pre-warned.

Nowadays, the big data equivalent of having your head blown off is probably the risk of data privacy fines or imprisonment and there is a bit more clarity around that which should avoid it happening in the first place.

However, the opportunity for big data gold is enormous. If you can think laterally about what information it would be useful to combine, get access to it, make the combinations happen, and then flog your products down the market then you are on to a right little earner.

You might even be on to a right little earner before you've produced the product because investment money can flow quite liberally when there is a sea of potential opportunity.

Of course, other people are thinking about doing the same thing so it's not easy to get there first. Creativity and imagination are useful additions to the melting pot though because that's what sparks the ideas for big data combos.

Now put your risk goggles on.

Could big data activity by others affect your business growth trajectory? If so, how? Which drivers of your success are impacted and which of those can you actually do something about? How will your customers change and who will your competitors be? In order to counter/exploit the deltas, do you need to take more risk or do you need to take less? Do you want to?

You might need to be pretty creative and imaginative when it comes to understanding the changes in risk levels to your business from activity inside and outside of it. Creative and imaginative business developments merit equally inspired risk management activity in support of great risk taking.

Increasingly, and accelerated by Covid-19, people are realizing how beneficial scenarios can be in putting handles on what could be done in alternative futures and what can be done now to improve agility in case particular scenarios occur.

Heads of Risk should really be pushing for this to take place in their organisations. In some industries, it would already be impossible to claim effective risk management if strategic risk scenarios had not already been explored in detail.

Maybe the leadership team behind Jurassic Park (the actual fictional park, if that's not too much of an oxymoron, not the movie) would have had longer careers if they had been more visionary and ingenious about managing risk well.

...and the cleaners would have had a lot less mess to clean up.

It can be okay to create a monster if you manage risk well

This is a big one.

One of the ways in which risk management can go wrong is where there is too much emphasis placed on risk avoidance. In those situations, people can start to think about risk management as being only about exerting increased control on risk.

I bet many readers of this book will have experienced this type of approach... they may even be skilled proponents of it.

The effect of this approach to risk management can be called risk minimization. For some, that might be a worthy goal but I'll wager that for most a better goal would be risk optimization because (at least in my book, if you'll pardon the pun) good risk management equals good risk taking.

Remember that before things went wrong, people were having a great time in Jurassic Park and even more so in Jurassic World sequel. Had risk been managed well, that fun might well have continued indefinitely.

If you are involved in managing risk, and when you think about it everyone is, please, please, please, PLEASE don't confuse yourself or others by always taking about risk management in a way which implies it's about minimizing risk.

Good risk management will help you build your monster and look after it in the right way. Whether it is a scary dinosaur created from DNA inside tree sap or whether it is a potentially even scarier big data monster created from other information sources, embrace risk management to help you succeed with it.

As a risk specialist, I say by all means go for it and if you are going to build the monster then make sure you manage risk appropriately. Thank you.

Some people find it entertaining to watch the most marvellous creations crumble due to poor risk management

There is opportunity as well as threat in Schadenfreude.

All but the very purest of us enjoy the occasional moments of Schadenfreude, don't we? I know I do!

Let me tell you a story about when I was younger - really young.

I was still at primary school and formed part of the school's music group which I think played its part in my life-long love of playing music in a way which is enjoyable and fun, even if not precisely as written down in the score.

The teacher who ran the music group (she was a genuinely lovely person) had used a bit of imagination to come up with the new concept for a performance we were going to undertake for the old folk somewhere. Although I can't remember what the name of it was, I can remember the location, the outside appearance of the building and the interior of the room we performed in just that once. The reason I still remember it, dear reader, will become apparent in the following tale of woe.

The deal was that we would play "Eye Level", the 1970s Simon Park Orchestra hit made famous as the theme tune to the television program "Van der Valk". If you don't know it, look it up on YouTube as it will help you enjoy this sad tale even more.

The music starts quietly and then builds fabulously before calming down towards the end.

As part of the creative concept, I was given a big cymbal and steel brush.

The idea was that in a hushed room full of expectant oldies, I'd kick things off by hitting the cymbal with the steel brush in a rhythmic way.

All I had to do was play Tah Ta-Ta-Tah over and over again until the orchestra joined in.

When I say, 'orchestra' I should probably explain a bit more. Don't laugh but we had a cassette tape with the hit record loaded onto it. The teacher had the biggest ghetto blaster she could carry up the stairs and the idea was that she would play that as a backing track for our music group's performance.

The music group itself (which was in its infancy at that stage and before she taught us how to play guitars in subsequent years etc), consisted of a largely, er, percussion section.

In addition to me on the big cymbal (by the way, I had a harder stick for the loud bits as well as the soft wire brush for the opening) we had specialists on tambourines, maracas, blocks, jingle bells and triangles. And let's not forget the glamorous 'front-men' in the kazoo section!

The plan was that slowly and surely, each of the instruments would join in as the piece progressed in keeping with the recorded backing track, and then fade out again towards the end so that at the very end it would just be me playing Tah Ta-Ta-Tah on the cymbal again until the music teacher gave the signal to stop and await the tumultuous applause which would no doubt follow.

Looking back, I can see why the teacher chose the backing track. If the victims, sorry, audience had to put up with us all hammering away in the way kids' music groups do then they might as well have something decent to listen to on the backing track!

Anyway, onto the stage we all shuffled and assumed our positions with a clear view of the audience. The music teacher, with her finger poised on the play button of the ghetto blaster, gave me the nod and off I went.

Tah Ta-Ta-Tah.

Tah Ta-Ta-Tah

Tah Ta-Ta-Tah

Tah Ta-Ta-Tah

'...that's strange', I thought '...it's normally started by now'.

Tah Ta-Ta-Tah

Tah Ta-Ta-Tah

At this point the teacher gave me the universal showbiz signal to keep going so with a few beads of sweat forming on my brow I did.

Tah Ta-Ta-Tah

Tah Ta-Ta-Tah

Tah Ta-Ta-Tah

I could see the teacher scrambling about checking the wires and could sense the mounting feeling of anxiety in everyone in the room - audience and 'orchestra'.

Tah Ta-Ta-Tah

Everyone except the teacher was now looking at me as the only person who was making a noise. For me it was excruciating!

Tah Ta-Ta-Tah

Tah Ta-T... wait - she gave me a less universal signal for me to stop.

'Sorry everyone, we are having a few problems with the technology'.

With a face as red as usually only the kazoo section would muster, it was with great relief that I put my arms down.

You quite enjoyed that little story didn't you? Go on, have a laugh at my expense why don't you? I told you people like a bit of Schadenfreude. I know, nobody got hurt in the physical sense but that experience has left it's scars on me I can tell you.

Although I can laugh at myself with you now, it is for bad reasons that I remember this particular little episode but it is funny how bad things can sometimes have a positive impact.

I mean, I probably was less worried about that sort of thing going wrong in the future because I had already experienced what it was like to be embarrassed like that (even though it wasn't my fault). For some, the result of such a 'humiliation' (maybe that's a bit strong but its how some kids would have felt it) would have been them never performing again. I was lucky though because although it left it's scars, it didn't put me off performing.

To this day, I love performing. Whether it is in a formal show or whether it is a different type of performance such as speaking at a conference, facilitating a workshop, recording a podcast, making a new business pitch, chairing a meeting etc, I love it. Sure, I sometimes get nervous and after a particular big or important performance I can sometimes get the shakes (funny how with me, the shaking happens after the performance rather than before or during!) but I genuinely love it.

Anyway, back to Schadenfreude and risk management failures.

Good risk taking means that sometimes you will win and sometimes you will lose and there is Schadenfreude opportunity for others when you lose.

Why did you lose though? Were you just unlucky or did your risk management fail meaning that your risk taking was not as good as you thought it was?

What actually is risk management failure because it surely can't be simply the occurrence of an adverse outcome although sometimes people argue that an adverse outcome must mean that risk management has failed - back to risk management school for them, I'd say.

Some people enjoy knocking risk management in this way.

"Risk Management has failed" they say, taking great delight in the opportunity for publicity it paves for them.

I live in a free country, though so here they are allowed to say that if they want.

The problem is that it implies that risk management as a discipline/specialism has failed rather than the more accurate interpretation that the management of risk in a particular situation as failed (poor risk management).

That sort of headline doesn't help those trying to improve risk management - especially when there is so much misunderstanding and under-education about what it is in the first place.

Some people find this all to be entertaining because they don't like change and therefore enjoy events which fairly or unfairly hinder risk management progress.

I think we have to accept that Schadenfreude exists in business - especially where there is internal competition so we simply need to be alert to it when it comes to risk management.

Whether others derive pleasure from unlucky occurrences or poor risk management, we probably need to allow them that but call them up on it if they make broader claims about failed risk management as a discipline.

The events in Jurassic Park were, after all, no reason to state that risk management doesn't work but they do instead provide lots of evidence (albeit fictional) that risk management sometimes needs to be better than it is and to that extent, the film series is an entertaining lesson in risk management.

If only I had thought of that when I had the conversation with Lord Attenborough because with all the risk related quotes in those films I think we could have gone on for quite a while talking about risk.

22

EEERM

LinkedIn article:

Do you think ERM should actually be spelled with three Es? Okay, maybe not but if I say there are three important Es associated with ERM would you be able to guess them?:

1) Existence. An easy one! It always exists in organisations. It's the degree of formality which varies
2) Efficiency. A little bit more sophistication is necessary to properly address this
3) Effectiveness. Smart thinking needed on the extent to which it supports the organisation in achieving it's goals.

Sometimes, people focus on (1) (most basic risk mgt textbooks will give you a good list of things which can be put in place) but it's (2) and (3) which bring value so it's important to be able to address both of them with competence, energy and intellectual rigour.

In their most sophisticated form, linked items (2) and (3) will be understood at a granular (ie specific tools, used by certain people, in specific underlying business processes and decision making) and also at more overarching levels.

In some situations, it's easy to see that an organisation (or division within it) has focused on Existence but not been particularly adept at addressing Efficiency and Effectiveness and that can lead to underperformance. Addressing all three Es seems important.

Pretty succinct, right?

Three Es, none of which represent the word that the actual E stands for (which is 'Enterprise'), which tell a tale.

During the crisis, some executives pulled their business continuity plans out of dusty cupboards and opened them for the first time - only to realise that they needed to be completely re-written.

They had previously fallen into the complacency trap associated with Existence... 'we have one of those already' and were finding out a bit late that it wasn't particularly good (effective/efficient).

Compliance with regulatory requirements is often measured by "existence" when it comes to risk management because supervisory gravity seems to pull firms in that direction. Sometimes that's helpful - especially when firms are well-behind where they should be in terms of a formalised approach to good risk taking and they need to understand all the components which are missing so that they can come up with a remediation plan.

However, in other situations, it really misses the point because existence is the starting point, not the end game! Unless risk management capability is effective then it might as well not exist and if it is going to exist then it might as well be efficient otherwise money will be wasted.

All the three Es article was really there to do was to remind everyone that effectiveness and efficiency are important and should be addressed.

It's such a simple message and it actually attracted some good public and private commentary from readers of the article.

I sometimes wonder why investors are not all over Effectiveness and Efficiency of risk management in the companies they invest in but that's for another article!

For now, just keep in mind the three Es and use them in your line of questioning of any risk management you see... you will come across to others as a lot smarter than you really are and we all like a bit of that now and again, don't we?!

The two main tips from this article are:
- Existence can be good but it is Effectiveness and Efficiency which bring value
- It is relatively easy to spot situations where the focus has been on Existence but not on Effectiveness or Efficiency

23

WHAT IF WE HAD…? STRATEGY, RISK, MAJOR PROGRAMS, BEHAVIOURAL CHANGE, INVESTOR INTEREST IN EFFECTIVE RISK MANAGEMENT

LinkedIn article:

…been thinking during these dark nights in London. Imagination can be powered when it's cold outside. I allowed my mind to wander, wonder and ponder to give some explorative headspace to "What if…?" questions. I came up with three for businesses and three for risk functions. I imagined the effect of some of these working in combination.

Here they are:

1. What if business strategies had a more sophisticated approach to dealing with the risks of and to those strategies and became more agile as a result?

2. What if the management of risk in and of projects was anchored to overall business success rather than completion of the tasks in scope of the projects alone?

3. What if all businesses and investors had a mature approach to discussing and managing true levels of risk and risk mgt effectiveness?

4. What if all risk functions were agile by design and in practice?

5. What if risk functions used behavioural change techniques in a more structured way to help those in the business manage risk more effectively?

6. What if risk functions helped the business clarify responsibility for risk without using sweeping generalisations such as three lines of defence terminology in situations where it leaves ambiguity?

What do you think and what would you add?

This was another of those short, bulleted posts I wrote when I was trying to work out whether articles or posts scored more highly on LinkedIn views. The deceptively simple items were grounded in a ton of first-hand experiences and observations from my long career and I knew that some of them do or could land quite big punches inside many organisations.

It was also another one of my writings where a casual reader might do a 'double take' because they might wonder why a 'What if...?' list contains things they might have assumed were already in place... many of which are explore in more detail elsewhere in this book.

As you will have seen from the intro, I wanted to make it not just of interest to risk functions but also to others in the business and that's why I came up with three items for the "business" and three items for the risk function. For clarity, a CEO would have an interest in all six.

The 'what if?' items are indeed written to lure readers into what might be some fantastical visions of possible futures only to lay out a series of items which it would seem difficult to argue against with the consequent embarrassment if businesses haven't at least formally considered having these things.

Of course, embarrassment is not a great sales strategy and instead it often leads to resistance and denial on behalf of the would-be client and frustration on behalf of the would-be Knight in shining armour.

Oh dear... obvious risk management improvement opportunities don't half kick up some problems, don't they?

Many organisations have the problem of 'the Emperor's new clothes' when it comes to the way they operate. Whether it be directly to do with the design of their risk management capability or the way in which risk is actually managed in the business, it can be difficult to point out that things might not be entirely as per the hushed and nodding masses.

To get to the promised land of optimized risk management, we need to navigate those problems which means time and effort and sometimes not inconsiderable personal risk for the person pushing for improvement.

At least they have logic on their side because it is really difficult to argue against having the items in the list. I suppose some acceptable excuses would include 'we are prioritizing other things' and that would be fair enough as long as the prioritization is sensible.

In many instances though, these possibilities will not have gone through a proper prioritization process. They are as they currently are because either nobody has suggested otherwise or they made a hash of it when they did try to bring about progress - no banana but at least they tried!

Although all six items in the article could form the basis for tips in themselves, I had a bit of a think about how best to encapsulate them in a single tip and it is this:

- Don't be embarrassed if a 'what if we had...?' is really a 'we should have...' - just do something about making it happen

24

THE DATA CHAIN MIGHT HAVE A WEAK LINK – DO YOU WANT TO USE IT?

LinkedIn article:

Let me tell you a secret. Opportunities to improve the strength of information flows around organisations are abundant. Okay, you might have been aware of that already but what is known to some people in some parts of an organisation can often be secret to those in other parts of the same organisation... by design but not intentionally (if that's not too much of a paradox to grapple with this early in an article).

The ability to see all of the opportunities from a single viewpoint is limited and that's because information crosses organisational silos and specialisms in a way that management structures typically don't. Whatever the subject of a particular information flow and whatever it's purpose, opportunities often remain untapped. The potential upside and downside of this can be very significant.

When considered end-to-end, there are often weak or missing links in data chains. It is not that the importance of accurate data is lost on people. Far from it - the value in having accurate data is increasingly understood in a (very) big data world where artificial intelligence is an increasingly important player in the Internet of Things (and people because they are in full control of the IOT).

People and organizations are spending, or rather *investing*, time and resources on improving the accuracy and reliability of their data. Of course when I say *their* data, that's not always the case either but that particular point is for another day.

"...all important links...in the chain...
but some get more attention than
others'

The work they are doing typically relates to closing gaps and addressing weak or missing links but the work that *is* being done is not really what I want to address in this article. It's the other problematic links in the chain that I want to draw attention to - ones which don't always get the attention they deserve or need.

Consider these 5 items below (the mis-numbering is intentional). They are all important links in the information chain but some get more attention than others with the result that some are weaker than others. Let's see if you agree with my assessment:

2) GET – Having the right architecture in place to get the data and to allow the information to flow from source systems etc is clearly important. The "wiring" needs to be right. As information opportunities arise, the wiring needs to be reconfigured to generate the data. Work being done here relates to new possibilities in terms of sources to pipe (not to mix my wires and pipes too much!) data from and also the way in which it is combined with other data. From my experience, this link tends to get a reasonable amount of time and attention spent (sorry, "invested") on it.

3) CHECK – Validation of the integrity of the data as well as the reliability of models used to process the data is clearly important too. Again, advances are being made in this area as new tools and approaches emerge to help. Clearly, the value of the information produced in the GET phase is underpinned by the confidence to be gained from the CHECK phase. Depending on the industry and in particular how heavily regulated it is, this link also gets a reasonable amount of attention.

"What is it about human nature which might influence the effectiveness... of reporting...?"

---

4) REPORT – Some people say that this is the same thing as GET. It might well be but it seems useful to separate it for the purposes of this article because there is and should be an art in reporting. How should the information be reported in order that it is properly understood? What is it about human nature (and increasingly artificial intelligence) which might influence the effectiveness of any particular style of reporting in any particular situation? In my experience, this aspect receives a lot less attention that GET and CHECK and yet it is a significant link in the information chain.

5) USE – What happens as a result? If REPORT is done well then people and machines will read the data reported and they will interpret it properly and understand the information in the way intended. What do they do with it, though? Is appropriate action taken as a result? This has always been important in organizations at different levels but is increasingly important in edge technology where information is channeled to very decentralised points in order that local decisions can be made quickly and reliably. Evidence at senior levels can be harder to produce. It's usually possible to point to examples of reports that have been used well to stimulate action but it's not so common to find a robust approach to ensuring

191

that all relevant information that has been reported is converted into action. Yet, if the actions are not taken as a result then what was the point of the GET, CHECK and REPORT phases in the first place?

1) WHAT - Finally, we have number one. What information would it be useful to produce? Who decides what information we should go and GET in the first place? In some instances, it will be the "bean counters". In some instances it will be regulatory supervisors. In some instances it will be investors. Increasingly, it might be artificial intelligence. The list goes on. We know what other people want us to produce but what do we want for ourselves? What will help us prospectively as we grow our business and deal with the new challenges that a shift to digital brings? Certainly, a properly developed strategy and strategy map will point the way to many pieces of information but such strategies and strategy maps are changing in quite a big way as a result of the digital shifts happening in the world. The need to monitor and predict has always been there but the need to do it in an increasingly uncertain business world means that uncertainty and risk should feature more highly. The need to build-in sensors is not something for hardware alone and this is a developing area too.

"...maybe this chain is in fact a cycle"

The USE phase provides more information to the WHAT phase and the WHAT phase feeds the GET phase so maybe this chain is in fact a cycle and that reinforces the importance of each link in the chain.

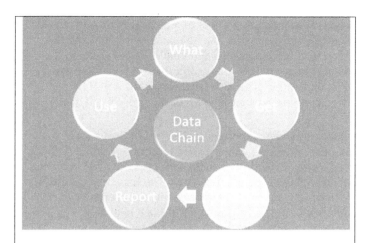

So far so good. The problem though is that silos exist in organizations even between people focused inside the same phase, let alone those responsible for the entire flow. Some organizations have some people responsible for all data in the same way as some organizations have some people responsible for all risks. Some will argue over the merits and demerits of such an approach. My own view is that these information chains (whether they are being used for risk information or other data) are possibly too numerous to be the responsibility of one person and the move to edge technology will make this even less feasible.

"...awareness of the whole chain... is important"

What will help then? There seems to be something about awareness of the whole chain which is important – that it is a chain in the first place, that it is a circular chain, that there is perhaps more to each link than it might at first appear, and that all the links need to be sufficiently strong. Whatever the subject of a particular data chain, if people operating inside one link can understand and appreciate the importance and challenges of those in the others then we will be onto something. There are times when that happens already, of course, but it will be increasingly important in the world of very big data.

Effective management requires effective flow of data. Effective risk management requires effective flow of risk data. Effective management of people risk requires effective flow of people risk data. The list could go on so we need to make sure that our chains are properly understood, in their entirety, by enough people as information flows evolve to serve the needs of our digitally shifting world.

Sometimes it's painful to see the bigger picture.

While everyone else is scurrying away in their own little corner, making components which look good to them, you are the one with line of sight of the whole and it doesn't look pretty. You will need to do something because otherwise, well, otherwise you will have an unbalanced product and some good effort in the corners will go to waste or at best be under-exploited.

That's pretty much what we have when it comes to risk information in many organisations.

Queue Samba music!

Da da dah,
Da da de dah.

Why Samba music? Well, when I first came up with the concept outlined in the article, it was in the build-up to the Olympics in Brazil which had also just hosted the Football World Cup.

Looking at my sketches for the concept in search of a title I could see that it was about...

...risk information flows... nah
...organizing risk information activity... nah
...risk information organizer... oh
...yes, Risk Information Organizer... RIO! Rio in Brazil!

Looking back, it wasn't the best descriptor for the concept but at least it was catchy!

I published this article about the subject after I left EY and a few years on, it's still pretty useful when it comes to understanding why risk information flows in organisations aren't everything they could be.

In some firms there are armies of enterprise architects making data flows possible and teams of quants addressing model validity and data integrity gets some good attention too.

That sounds like a lot of good activity going on doesn't it? And indeed it is... which should help bring about better risk taking. Bravo!

What about the other three stages though? After all, if you agree with the article that it is a chain and for that matter a circular one, then those other phases need to be equally strong, right?

The disappointing reality in many firms is that the other phases don't get the time and attention they deserve because nobody has though of things in this way.

One of the things I still do as an independent consultant is Board and Management Effectiveness reviews and a key part of those evaluations relate to risk information.

In all but the worst firms, GET and CHECK score highly but the other three less so.

Why is that? How can it be?

Maybe one reason is the lack of understanding of what good looks like in the WHAT, REPORT and USE phases. That might be exacerbated due to the fact that they should be different in different organisations. Great design doesn't mean that everything is designed the same way.

More examples of what good looks like in those three phases would probably be helpful to some.

I think there could be a more proximate trigger though and that is simply the understanding of the circular chain and the phases which sit within it.

Think about information which flows through your own organization or if you are independent then an organization you are familiar with. Start with the GET phase and think about who makes sure that's done well. Then do the same for CHECK.

Now think about the REPORT, USE and WHAT phases. Do you think they could be better?

For some pieces of risk information you might say 'no, everything's fine thank you Clive' and you might well be right as there are always some exceptions.

I bet you if you make enough effort though, you will see opportunity for the sorts of improvements the article points to in one of the three other phases. You might even see and accept that the value of work undertaken in the GET/ CHECK phases is actually undermined by the lack of attention given to the others.

I don't want you to have to work too hard though because this book is supposed to be accessible and fun so let's just say that 'I will love it' (as Kevin Keegan once famously blurted out) if you could commit the five phases to memory and used it any time you are thinking about risk information flows in your organization because that way it really is likely to help better risk decisions and consequent better risk taking.

The best points to summarise from this chapter are probably:

- Get and check your risk information but don't forget the art of reporting it, ensuring its use for decision making and it's role in further thinking about what to gather in the first place.
- Risk information data chains are cycles
- Make a point at looking at all five phases when you are trying to work out where the weakest links are

25

HISTORY... A DEFIANT CONSTRAINT ON CORPORATE
AMBITION – AND HOW A LITTLE BEHAVIOUR CHAIN
MIGHT HELP

LinkedIn article:

Let me ask you this...

How easy do you find it to get people to do things differently? Relax, it can be tricky for all of us.

What about behavioral change and associated techniques? How easy is it to get others to use behavioral change techniques in their own efforts to achieve business change?

Frequently, people find it difficult to persuade others to use behavioral assessment and change techniques. Whether it is a major change program, a risk management initiative, a concerted effort to change culture or broader execution of strategy, those who know about the techniques can sometimes struggle to get those in positions of power to adopt them.

How can that be? After all, although there is some debate about the merits of particular techniques, the logic seems clear for others and yet they are not always used when it might be useful to do so.

The Challenge

Often, the difficulty encountered is *"because we've not done it that way in the past"*.

"We didn't do it that way last time".

"I don't know anybody who has done it that way before".

Ah yes, history – a defiant constraint on corporate ambition… a foil of future focus… a destroyer of… well you get my point!

This is not just a problem for those seeking adoption of behavioral change techniques, of course. Anyone trying to convince others to adopt new ways of working needs to address the *"we've not done it that way before"* syndrome until such time as the tipping point is reached and adoption becomes the norm.

Imagine the terrible progress the human race would have made though phrases like *"we've never done it that way before"* were enough to put us off trying to advance things.

It's often tempting to back down, isn't it? A quieter life can sometimes be achieved by going along with those who would prefer to do things as they have done in the past. In the long run, where does that get us collectively, though? Sometimes, the old way is best – it would be foolish to pretend otherwise but there are occasions where it would be better for everyone if a new approach was adopted.

An intervention which is often overlooked

For those whose focus is to try and encourage others to consider and use behavioral change techniques (we'll skip the issue of who that should be because that in itself is worthy of a separate article), this dilemma is common. For that sort of change, there is perhaps a little chain of

199

events that could do with an intervention which is often overlooked.

Think for a minute... "I want to convince someone to use behavioral change techniques more often so how should I do that? How should I go about convincing them there is a better way to operate?"

What are your options? Well, you could shout at them (metaphorically or actually, if you prefer). I wonder how well that might work? In some situations, shouting might work. In some situations the desired change will occur as a result. You might be lucky.

Is there anything better than shouting?

Wait a minute, though. Are there other behavioral change techniques available which could be more reliable and effective than shouting in certain situations?

Yes, there are.

Should I use them when I try to convince others to use them?

Maybe you should.

...and there is the little chain intervention I mentioned. Conscious consideration and use of the right behavioral change techniques in initial dialogue could be the best way to get others to use the behavioral change techniques in managing risk and implementing strategy. The better the use in the initial chain of communication, the better the chance of adoption in the business and the better the organizational outcome which will empower more advanced use in due course.

It's often missing in dialogue between those who understand behavioral change techniques and program managers, business unit leaders, strategic planners, risk managers etc which could be one reason why history is often such a difficult constraint on achieving desired behavioral change.

Be ready

So, the next time you are in a conversation with someone about trying to get others to use behavioral change techniques and they ask you which techniques you are using in the first place in order to influence those people in power, you will have your answer ready won't you?

Hands up everyone who uses behavioural change techniques. Let me see those hands in the air. Browning, Jones, Simpkins, you at the back... hands up.

Everyone should have their hands up in the air right now... everyone. We all use at least some of them one way or another even if it is shouting at the kids or screaming at your parents.... that sort of thing. So come on, everybody - hands in the air and while they are all up lets wave them about a bit and have a sing song.

To the left... to the right... to the left again.

Okay, that's enough you can put them down now.

If everybody already uses behavioural change techniques then why did I feel the need to write this article?

It's because we often don't realise we are doing it. We know we are trying to bring about a change but we don't always realise that we are using a verified behavioural change technique to do so.

We are, as some might say, unconsciously competent some of the time and unconsciously incompetent some of the time.

What I'd like to see is people being more consciously competent more of the time when it comes to using behavioural change techniques for the purposes of improving risk taking. If that involves some intermediate stops at the consciously incompetent station then so be it (because self-awareness can be a very powerful tool, in the right hands).

Increasingly, I see people trying to get others in organisations to formally consider the use of well-established behavioural change techniques to bring about changes in the sorts of areas listed in the article. That's great... really great.

The reasons they sometimes fail though is because they haven't been smart about using those techniques when it comes to influencing key people in the first place.

I'm not saying that all behavioural change techniques should be used all of the time but I do think it worth thinking in a structured way about the possibility of using them when you are trying to have the influence you seek.

Influence is an amazing thing to have. Throughout my leadership journey, I received lots of great tips about how to gain it and use it.

One of the most useful ones I ever received was 'you need to be interested to be interesting'. If you are not naturally a networker in social situations and, like most people, struggle to initiate discussions then this is the sort of tip which you will find very helpful but, like the other tips in the book, it's only helpful if you use it.

I suppose if I really think about it, if there is one tip which before all others I would give to those trying to bring about risk management improvement (ie better risk taking) then it would relate to the use of behavioural change techniques as those offer keys to the locked doors guarding the existing modus operandi.

In recent years, at risk management conference and the like, there has been increasing coverage of what drives behaviour in individuals and related factors such as unconscious bias etc.

For some this is totally new. For a few others such as me who studied organizational behaviour as part of their risk management studies over 30 years ago, it doesn't feel so fresh although the increased recognition of it as being useful to those driving forward risk management is indeed refreshing.

But while there is more attention being given to what drives peoples risk taking behaviour, there is not so much being given to how Heads of Risk should use behavioural change techniques themselves for the benefit of their organization.

Whenever I conduct a risk management effectiveness review nowadays, I always ask for evidence that behavioural change techniques have been considered (and typically used) when trying to bring about risk management improvements. I find it to be a good marker of the maturity of risk management capability in the organization and of the likelihood of planned initiatives succeeding.

Asking the Head of Risk about which behavioural change techniques he himself is using in order to influence others into using them usually reveals something useful for both parties too.

In terms of risk management tips from this chapter then, I'd say they could best be described as:
- Don't be discouraged from progress by those stuck in the past

- Don't expect them to see the light and switch easily without influence from you
- Behavioural change techniques are not just for others to use

EPILOGUE

There you have it, folks - I've done my best to make our little risk management mystery tour fun as well as insightful and I really hope you enjoyed it and would love to hear from you.

Whether you agreed with all, many, some or none of my tips, I hope that at least one phrase, point or concept in these pages has sparked an idea or energized you to do something more about better, improved risk taking in your work lives and maybe in your personal lives too.

Everyone knows that the future is uncertain and Covid19 gave us all a reminder of just how uncertain our future can be. More uncertainty and opportunity awaits us from other things lurking around the corner... that's what being alive is all about but our responses to risk don't all need to be the same.

Those who know more about risk management in a formal sense, might be better placed to deal with these uncertainties and take the opportunities than those who don't.

And what about those who can help others learn more about risk management in new and imaginative ways?

You decide.

ABOUT THE AUTHOR

Born in the United Kingdom not far from the birthplace of Victorian explorer David Livingstone (of 'Livingstone, I presume' fame), Clive Martin moved to London (and not far from the Queen) in 1990 after graduating with Distinction in Risk Management at the only place in Europe you could do it in those days.

He set about building his career serving large clients with Willis (now Willis Towers Watson) at the same time as discovering the delights of London's West End.

He continued his career at The Peninsular and Oriental Steam Navigation Company when it was a major global conglomerate headquartered in Pall Mall (even nearer the Queen) before joining EY (further away from the Queen but nearer the Prime Minister).

He rose through the ranks at Ernst & Young where he stayed for 17 years including 9 as a full Partner before working independently and in collaboration with others in the gig economy.

Operating mainly in New York, London and Zurich, Clive's client base extends across all major branches of financial services and other industries including energy, hospitality and education and he has a successful track record of managing large client accounts, running interdisciplinary projects and setting and implementing strategy for different types of professional services practices.

Leading highly skilled, diverse and motivated teams in different specialisms, he has throughout his career contributed risk management thought leadership in various forms including conferences, podcasts, journals, newspapers, magazines and social media.

Clive is a Certified Fellow of the Institute of Risk Management and a Fellow of the Chartered Insurance

Institute but has lost his school education certificates and says he can't remember what he got in his school exams.

He lives with his family in South West London where they all cheerily put up with his art creations and music recitals as well as his, occasionally frenzied, typing.

Printed in Great Britain
by Amazon

56108021R00129